The Hallelujah Highway

# Font and Table Series

The Font and Table Series offers pastoral perspectives on Christian baptism, confirmation and eucharist.

Other titles in the series:

A Catechumenate Needs Everybody: Study Guides for Parish Ministers

At That Time: Cycles and Seasons in the Life of a Christian

Baptism Is a Beginning

The Catechumenate and the Law

Celebrating the Rites of Adult Initiation: Pastoral Reflections

The Church Speaks about Sacraments with Children: Baptism, Confirmation, Eucharist, Penance

Confirmed as Children, Affirmed as Teens

Finding and Forming Sponsors and Grandparents

Guide for Sponsors

How Does a Person Become a Catholic?

How to Form a Catechumenate Team

Infant Baptism: A Parish Celebration

Issues in the Christian Initiation of Children

One at the Table: The Reception of Baptized Christians

Readings in the Christian Initiation of Children

Welcoming the New Catholic

Confirmation: A Parish Celebration

Related materials available through Liturgy Training Publications:

The Rite of Christian Initiation of Adults (ritual and study editions)

Rito de la Iniciación Cristiana de Adultos (ritual and study editions)

Catechumenate: A Journal of Christian Initiation

Baptism Sourcebook

Forum Essays series:

The Role of the Assembly in Christian Initiation

Eucharist as Sacrament of Initiation

On the Rite of Election

Preaching the Rites of Christian Initiation

Liturgical Spirituality and the Rite of Christian Initiation of Adults

The Hallelujah Highway

A History of the Catechumenate

PAUL TURNER

LITURGY
TRAINING
PUBLICATIONS

ACKNOWLEDGMENTS

This book was edited by Victoria M. Tufano; Audrey Novak Riley was the production editor, with assistance from Gabriela Ruelas and Theresa Pincich. Larry Cope designed the book, and Karen Mitchell typeset it in Palatino and Friz Quadrata. It was printed by Worzalla in Stevens Point, Wisconsin. The index was created by Mary Laur.

Photo research was done by Julie Laffin of Peter Cook, Inc., of Riverside, Illinois, and Reverend John Render, CP, of the Passionist Research Center in Chicago.

Cover photo © 2000 Bob Krist/Tony Stone Images. Maps © 1998 Digital Wisdom, Inc.

Scripture texts used in this work are taken from the New Revised Standard Version, © 1989 Division of Christian Education of the National Council of Churches of Christ in the United States of America. All rights reserved.

Excerpts from the English translation of the *Rite of Christian Initiation of Adults* © 1985, International Committee on English in the Liturgy. All rights reserved. Used with permission.

THE HALLELUJAH HIGHWAY: A HISTORY OF THE CATECHUMENATE © 2000, Archdiocese of Chicago: Liturgy Training Publications, 1800 North Hermitage Avenue, Chicago IL 60622-1101; 1-800-933-1800; fax 1-800-933-7094; e-mail orders@ltp.org. Visit our website at www.ltp.org. All rights reserved.

Library of Congress Cataloging-in-Publication Data
Turner, Paul, 1953–
   The hallelujah highway : a history of the catechumenate / Paul Turner.
       p. cm.
   Includes bibliographical references and index.
       1. Catechumens—History. 2. Baptism—Catholic Church—History. 3. Initiation rites—Religious aspects—Catholic Church—History of doctrines. I. Title.
   BX935 .T88 2000
   264'.020813—dc21
                                                                                    00-057135

1-56854-320-4

HWY

04 03 02 01 00   5 4 3 2 1

Whoever desires the baptism of Christ
chooses a new life. . . .

Let's pack up our provisions—our faith as well as the cross.
Let's catch the boat and get on board.
Don't forget the anchor, the hope of our salvation. . . .

May the grace of Christ, our protector, accompany us;
let us sweetly sing our traveling song,

"Hallelujah!"

so that, joyful and protected, we may enter
our eternal and most happy homeland.

—Quodvultdeus of Carthage (+ 454)
The New Song 1:1, 2:4, 2:9

Contents

I wish to thank
Michael Driscoll, who welcomed
The Hesburgh Library
        at the University of Notre Dame, which saved
Vicky Tufano, who asked
James Comiskey, who substituted
Bishop Raymond Boland, who agreed
Maxwell Johnson, who advised
Michael Witczak, who read
Eleanor Bernstein, who provided
Tim Fitzgerald, who diverted
Joe Kempf, who prayed
God, who guides the journey.

IULIO AC RACHELI MEYER

A QVIBVS SVM SACRO EX FONTE SVSCEPTVS

DIV CONDITIS

NVMQVAM OBLITIS

SEMPER QVIBVS AD ARAM CONIVNGOR

Me ◆ 1
Author and Pastor

The journey of faith traverses a highway of temptation and grace. For Christians, it rises through a period called the catechumenate, and delivers its travelers safely home with baptism.

Paul Turner baptizing.

The catechumenate is an apprenticeship for life as a Christian. Catechumens turn from unbelief to belief, from darkness to light, from silence to song, and from life outside the community to participation in the body of Christ. The history of the catechumenate is inescapably a story about people. And a story about the living Son of God.

Let me tell you a story about the catechumenate. It's not the whole story; that would take too many books. It's not about every Christian church; it will follow the developments in Roman Catholicism. It's not about the baptism of infants who receive confirmation and communion much later. And the people we call "candidates"—those baptized but never catechized, or those baptized in one church who make a profession of faith in another? It's not about them. It's about unbaptized adults who seek the gift of faith and sing a joyful song at journey's end. This story is about the preparation for and celebration of adult baptism in the Catholic church.

Me, I was baptized as an infant. Three days after I was born. My parents could tell I was a sinner from the start. So you might think this story isn't about me. You could say that. But in another way it is. Know what? It's also about you.

Peter ◆2
Disciple and Evangelist

The sound started in the skies. Roaring, whistling like a driving wind, its tones rattled the walls and filled the room with its thunder. It shook the floor, the chairs, and even those who sat in them. The disciples of Jesus, fearful already because of his absence, clustered as one community since they had shared one experience. They were headless now since he had ascended to those very skies from which these terrible timbres rang forth, headless but for one among them who had led their discipleship with Jesus through faith and fear, through service and resistance, one upon whom rested their hopes to harness the future and bring them rebirth: Peter.

Art Resource.

St. Peter Baptizing the Neophytes by Massaccio (1401–28), Brancacci Chapel, Santa Maria de Carmine, Florence, Italy.

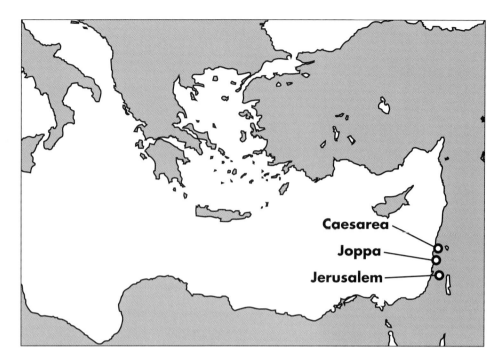

The sound seized them all and translated their speech into many languages. They opened their mouths in praise of God's wonder, and the sound poured forth onto the ears of bystanders amazed at hearing their own language, understanding what they never could before. "How do they do that?" they wondered. "What does this mean?"

Then Peter stood. He raised his voice, and the sound came forth anew, a deafening declaration: "Jesus of Nazareth was a man whom God sent to you with miracles, wonders, and signs. God has raised up this Jesus and we are his witnesses."

"What are we to do?" the onlookers asked.

"Repent and be baptized, receive forgiveness and the Holy Spirit."

Three thousand accepted the call to baptism that very day. Then they entered the community of the faithful and shared instruction, charity and eucharist.

Then Philip began to speak, and starting with this scripture, he proclaimed to the Ethiopian eunuch the good news about Jesus. As they were going along the road, they came to some water; and the eunuch said, "Look, here is water! What is to prevent me from being baptized?" He commanded the chariot to stop, and both of them, Philip and the eunuch, went down into the water, and Philip baptized him. Acts of the Apostles 8:35–38

Eventually Peter sought hospitality at the quiet home of Simon the Tanner at Joppa, and yet he felt disquieted. He asked for food, but then entered a trance that convinced him that God was calling not just Jews but Gentiles, too, to belief in Jesus.

A knock at the door disturbed Peter's prayer. He saw across the threshold three visitors who had come from the Gentile household of Cornelius, a centurion from Caesarea. "Cornelius is upright and God-fearing," they testified, "highly esteemed by the Jewish community. An angel had him summon you for instruction."

Immediately Peter journeyed toward their home. Cornelius met Peter outside his house. Peter entered with him.

"Why have you sent for me?"

"To hear what God has given you," the centurion replied.

Peter addressed the household: "God anointed Jesus of Nazareth with the Holy Spirit and with power. He is judge of the living and the dead."

But the sound of Peter's voice was overpowered by the sound that returned from the heavens. The Holy Spirit fell upon them in that house at Caesarea as happened on Pentecost in the upper room at Jerusalem.

"What should keep them from baptism?" Peter reasoned. He commanded that Cornelius and his household be baptized in the name of the Lord Jesus.

Peter stayed there several days so they could hear in many ways the sound of the word of God.

These stories from the Acts of the Apostles (2:1–41; 10:1—11:18) concern the administration of baptism under the guidance of Peter. But more, they reveal the interests of the first-century church regarding baptism and its preparation.

The Acts of the Apostles comes from the author of Luke's gospel. The two books were written probably about the year 80. They circulated first as anonymous works; later the author was given the name *Luke*. They record events recalled by believers. Although the full accuracy of historic detail cannot be substantiated, these stories reveal the faith of the writer's community, and that people in the apostolic church advanced through several stages toward baptism.

FIRST INTEREST

Both stories explain that people first expressed interest in following Christ after having an unusual spiritual experience. At Pentecost, Jews who had come to Jerusalem from many countries each heard their own language spoken by those who did not know it. In Caesarea, Cornelius had a vision of an angel while praying.

PREPARATION FOR BAPTISM

In both incidents people asked for enlightenment. Those who witnessed the miracle of languages at Jerusalem asked, "What does this mean?" In Caesarea, Peter received a request for instruction. If the Christian community that first told these stories began their catechetical sessions with a question (for example, "What does this mean?", "What are we to do?" or "Why have you sent for me?"), that technique may have shaped the written form of these dialogues.

Cornelius strengthened his case with testimony. Two slaves and a soldier bore witness to Peter while standing at the threshold of a house. The incident acknowledges the community's responsibility for discerning the proper disposition for baptism. It also suggests the ritual significance of a threshold.

Both at Pentecost and at the home of Cornelius, Peter delivered an instruction that proclaimed Jesus. The same approach appears also in Peter's discourse at Solomon's portico (Acts 3:11–26) and in Philip's conversation with an Ethiopian eunuch (Acts 8:26–40).

Conversion preceded baptism. Peter invited his listeners in Jerusalem to repentance, to turn from their former way of life and accept Jesus. Their conversion moved them from being "no people" to being "God's people" (1 Peter 2:10). At

Cornelius' house, that conversion became evident in a powerful way: The Holy Spirit fell upon the group as at Pentecost.

In some cases, a leader then made a decision in favor of baptism. When Peter realized that Gentiles in Caesarea now stood among God's elect, he authorized their baptism. His question, "What can keep them from being baptized?" resembles the one the Ethiopian posed to Philip, "What is to keep me from being baptized?" That same question may have been used in the early Christian community to obtain final testimony, or to be left unanswered as a rhetorical affirmation that the time for baptism had come.

BAPTISM

In Jerusalem and in Caesarea, baptism immediately followed the proclamation of the gospel; the period of formation was astoundingly brief. The same brief interval emerges in Philip's conversion of the Ethiopian and in the story that precedes it: A group turned from magic to baptism after hearing Philip's proclamation and witnessing miracles (Acts 8:9–13). However, these abrupt accounts presume a larger context. Cornelius had been preparing his Gentile heart even

They devoted themselves to the apostles' teaching and fellowship, to the breaking of bread and the prayers.

Acts 2:42

before he met Peter; the Jews requesting baptism already possessed a lifetime of religious experience. The proximity of instruction and initiation in these stories demonstrates the interdependence of proclamation and rebirth (cf. 1 Peter 1:22–25).

In Acts, those baptized at a single event ranged in number from individuals to households to thousands. Surely the one baptizing spoke some words, but the formula may have varied. In Caesarea, Peter ordered baptism "in the name of the Lord Jesus." At the close of Matthew's gospel Jesus commanded, "Baptize in the name of the Father and of the Son and of the Holy Spirit" (28:19). Either or both of these may represent baptismal formulas from the early church.

The word *baptize* comes from a Greek verb meaning *dip;* the term probably described a complete immersion into water. In fact, the Exodus from Egypt served as an image for Christian baptism (1 Peter 1:13–21), as did the flood of Noah (1 Peter 3:20–21). It would be reasonable to assume that the three thousand who heard the message in Jerusalem were already outdoors and so were baptized in some public water source, and that the household of Cornelius were baptized in their home. Philip baptized the Ethiopian in a pool of water.

LIFE AFTER INITIATION

After the Pentecost baptism, people devoted themselves to community life, instruction and prayer (Acts 2:42). The household of Cornelius asked Peter to stay with them a few days. In one instance Peter and John imposed hands on a group already baptized by the deacon Philip (Acts 8:14–17). Those who accepted baptism were expected to reject their former sin and crave "spiritual milk" like newborns (1 Peter 2:1–2).

◆◆◆

From stories about Peter some assumptions can be made about baptism in the apostolic church.

First Interest

• Some spiritual experience attracted the attention of unbelievers.

Preparation for Baptism

• People demonstrated their receptivity to instruction by asking questions, providing testimony, or standing at a threshold.

• Instruction centered on Jesus.

• People expressed their conversion by repentance.

• A leader decided that baptism should take place.

Baptism

• Baptism followed a brief period of formation.

• Baptism probably took place by immersion wherever a water source was available, either in homes or outdoors.

• The number of people baptized at one time varied, from individuals or small groups to large numbers.

• The minister probably spoke a formula of words.

Life after Initiation

• After baptism people lived in community and observed a common moral code, sharing instruction and eucharist.

• Handlaying followed at least one instance of baptism.

3 ◆ Paul
Opponent and Apostle

The light leapt from the heavens. It struck Saul so intensely that he fell to the ground, unable to see. Surrounded by his companions in the noonday sun, the fallen man heard the sound, "Saul, Saul, why are you persecuting me?"

Baptism of St. Paul, Cappella Palatina, Palazzo Reale, Palermo, Italy.

Saul, a zealous believer in Israel's God, had obtained papers authorizing him to terrorize the disciples of Jesus in Damascus, to arrest women and men alike and haul them captive to Jerusalem.

Then this.

Blind, helpless but for the support of his companions, he entered the city of Damascus not as prosecutor, but as pauper. While fasting for three days, he prayed for deliverance.

The disciple Ananias laid hands on him, and light entered Saul's eyes. He received baptism, forgiveness and a new name, Paul. He remained in Damascus with the very disciples he had come to apprehend, and began to preach that Jesus was the son of God.

Paul inspired many other people to seek baptism. At the riverbank in Philippi, Paul and his companions preached to a group of women. Among them was Lydia, a dealer in purple goods from Thyatira. The Lord opened her heart, and she accepted Paul's message. She was baptized with her household.

Paul and his companions stayed with Lydia until he and Silas were arrested for disturbing the peace. Chained to a stake and under guard, they were set free from prison by a violent earthquake. The jailer, filled with fear, called for light. Seeing Paul and Silas he asked, "What must I do to be saved?" "Believe in the Lord Jesus," they responded. Paul instructed the jailer's entire household, and in the dark of night they all accepted baptism. They dined together and celebrated their faith in God.

In Corinth many of those who heard Paul preach during his eighteen months there believed and were baptized. At Ephesus he spoke to a group of twelve about Jesus, and they were baptized. When he laid hands on them, the Holy Spirit came down upon them. Gradually the light that filled Paul at his own conversion illumined the hearts of countless believers.

Wherever Paul went, baptism followed. It sealed his own conversion (Acts of the Apostles 9:1–22; 22:6–16). It steered his ministry (Acts 16:13–15; 16:25–34; 18:8–11; 19:1–7; 1 Corinthians 1:14–16). It surfaced in his letters. (Scholars dispute the authorship of some of the letters, which are thought to date from the 50s and 60s.)

FIRST INTEREST

The stages of baptism indicated by the stories about Peter corroborate the testimony about Paul. People first expressed interest in the gospel due to some spiritual experience. Paul himself was blinded and heard the voice of Jesus. Lydia was already at a place of prayer. The jailer was terrified by an earthquake. The disciples in Ephesus had already accepted the baptism of John.

PREPARATION FOR BAPTISM

Formation often began with a formal request. Paul asked, "What must I do?" (Acts 22:10). The jailer wondered the same: "What must I do to be saved?" This question already appeared at Pentecost (Acts 2:37). It also shows up in the gospels. The crowds ask John the Baptist, "What should we do?" (Luke 3:10), and the rich young man asks Jesus, "What must I do to inherit eternal life?" (Luke 18:18; cf.

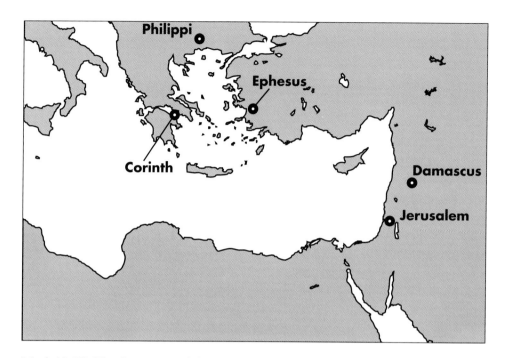

Mark 10:17). The frequency of the question, especially in works by Luke, suggests its use in a catechetical format familiar to him.

The testimony of the community also surfaces, though not as directly as it did for Cornelius. In fact, Ananias hesitates to instruct Saul because he has received such damaging testimony from the Christian community (Acts 9:8). Still, the companions who physically support the blind Saul (9:13) paint a picture of the help required in the pursuit of faith. Ultimately, God bears testimony for Saul (9:15).

Paul prepared people for baptism by preaching conversion. He called Jews and Gentiles to repentance and belief (Acts 13:38; 20:20–21). In his letters to faithful Christians he identified the kind of conversion they had undergone: He spoke of those freed from slavery to sin under the law (Romans 6:17) and of those who renounced cosmic forces (Colossians 2:20). He reminded Gentiles how they turned from their idols to worship the one true God (1 Thessalonians 1:9–10). Paul expected people to renounce their former allegiance and to believe in Christ.

That belief in Christ burst forth in short statements throughout the letters of Paul and elsewhere in the New Testament. "Jesus is Lord" (1 Corinthians 12:3; Philippians 2:11), says Paul. "There is one Lord, one faith, one baptism" (Ephesians 4:5). He preached Christ raised from the dead (1 Corinthians 15:12), God's mystery revealed (Romans 16:25), and salvation for those who believed it (Romans 10:9). John also distinguished those who deny and those who acknowledge the Son (1 John 2:23). Leaders exhorted people to believe in the name of God's Son (John 3:18; Acts 10:43; 1 John 5:13). In Mark's gospel Jesus promises salvation to those who believe in the good news and accept baptism (16:16). In a later edition of the story of the Ethiopian, Philip draws this affirmation of faith from his new disciple: "I believe that Jesus Christ is the Son of God" (Acts 8:37). Such statements expressed the faith that preaching intended to evoke.

Those who desired discipleship also expressed their conversion by their behavior. Paul fasted for three days (Acts 9:9). The jailer bathed the wounds of his former prisoners (Acts 16:33). Idolaters, adulterers, thieves and others forsook their ways (1 Corinthians 6:9–11). Gentiles, however, did not have to become Jews before becoming Christians (Acts 15:28–29).

Ritual prayer may also have accompanied baptismal preparation. Before Ananias baptized Saul, he imposed hands to bestow sight and to fill him with the Holy Spirit (Acts 9:17–18; 22:12–16). This gesture brought physical healing, but it also presaged spiritual enlightenment. This story may also indicate that the primitive church practiced handlaying before baptism. Support for this theory comes from a related story (Mark 7:31–37) in which some people brought Jesus a deaf man with a speech impediment and asked him to lay his hand on him. Jesus took the man away, put his fingers into the deaf ears and touched the impaired tongue with his spittle. Looking up to heaven, Jesus groaned, *"Ephphetha,"* which means "Be opened." The man was cured.

Throughout this odd procedure, the details that parallel the approach to baptism are striking. The story is situated between the two miracles of the loaves (6:34–44 and 8:1–9), which prefigure the eucharist. This unit of stories is followed by the healing of a blind man (8:22–25) who is also brought to Jesus for his touch, and who receives welcome and healing apart from the crowd. Most remarkable is the preservation of the Aramaic word *ephphetha,* indicating the antiquity of the story and the tenacity in other translations of a technical word prized by the community.

In this miracle, as in the story of Saul, some people representing the community sought handlaying and a cure for an impaired man whom they brought to a healer who prayed, who took the man away from the crowd, and who produced physical and spiritual benefits. Other accounts of Jesus healing the blind (for instance, John 9:1–41; Mark 10:46–52) play on the same metaphor of receiving the eyes of faith. It is possible that a similar ritual, complete with the use of the Aramaic word, was already in use by the primitive Christian community for those seeking baptism.

The length of time in preparation for baptism remained brief. Paul spent three days with Ananias before his own baptism. Lydia, the jailer, their households and others received baptism after a short catechesis. According to Acts, Paul stayed in Corinth a year and a half (18:11) and in Rome for two years (28:30); that provided ample time for many individuals and groups to accept Christ.

BAPTISM

Paul gives no direct record of the words used in baptism, although his disciples in Ephesus were baptized in the name of Jesus (Acts 19:5) so the believers could receive the Holy Spirit. He reminds the Corinthians that they were baptized in the name of Jesus and in the Spirit (1 Corinthians 6:11). The application of baptism to a sacred name explains the divisions in Corinth caused by allegiance to ministers

On the sabbath day we went outside the gate by the river, where we supposed there was a place of prayer; and we sat down and spoke to the women who had gathered there. A certain woman named Lydia, a worshiper of God, was listening to us; she was from the city of Thyatira and a dealer in purple cloth. The Lord opened her heart to listen eagerly to what was said by Paul. When she and her household were baptized, she urged us, saying, "If you have judged me to be faithful to the Lord, come and stay at my home." And she prevailed upon us. Acts 16:13–15

© 2000 Passionist Research Center.

Temple at Corinth.

(1 Corinthians 1:12–15). For Paul, baptism "in the name of Jesus" may refer more to acceptance of Jesus than to a formula of words.

By its definition, baptism involves water. Paul designated it a "bath" (Ephesians 5:26), a "new birth" (Titus 3:5), and he named the baptized "washed" (1 Corinthians 6:11). He compared baptism to the Exodus (1 Corinthians 10:1–2). These images assume that baptism was administered with a quantity of water.

Paul's rich metaphors opened a fertile vocabulary for baptism. He called it a death and resurrection with Christ (Romans 6:1–11; Colossians 2:12), reminiscent of Jesus' injunction to Nicodemus that one must be born again to have eternal life (John 3:3, 5). Following his own baptism, Paul assumed a new name. He spoke of the anointing and sealing of the Christian (2 Corinthians 1:21–22; Ephesians 1:13; 4:30). He said the baptized were clothed with Christ (Galatians 3:27; cf. Romans 13:14; Ephesians 4:22–24; Colossians 3:9–12) and urged them to accept the light of Christ (Romans 13:12; Ephesians 5:14). The letter to the Hebrews suggests that handlaying formed part of the early Christian liturgy (6:2). In one episode (Acts 19:1–6), Paul laid hands on a newly baptized group. Although Paul probed these metaphors and gestures to unfurl the meaning of baptism, the regular introduction of naming, anointing, clothing, light and handlaying into baptismal rituals came later.

LIFE AFTER INITIATION

After baptism, Christians were expected to live what they believed. Virtually every letter of Paul exhorts the readers to Christlike behavior. Most importantly, those who professed faith in Christ were to abstain from the cup of idol worship while they partook in the communion cup of Christ (1 Corinthians 10:20–21).

By stitching together threads from the life of Paul, a picture of baptism and its preparation emerges. The evidence does not suffice, however, to conclude that initiation commonly included most or all of these elements. Still, the scriptures support the assumption that people joined the Christian community through stages of instruction and prayer. The tenth chapter of Luke's gospel will tempt the historian of baptismal preparation to see a progression foreshadowing the catechumenate: Jesus gives an instruction on discipleship (1–15), asserts the value of welcome (16), proclaims the impotence of Satan (17–19), affirms the inscription of the disciples' names in heaven (20), and blesses eyes and ears (21–24). All this is followed by the parable of the Good Samaritan, which opens (25) with the question,

"What must I do?" The catechumenate, as such, was still to develop, but its seeds were planted in the apostolic ministry of the New Testament.

◆◆◆

In the ministry of Paul some elements of baptismal ministry may be observed.

First Interest

- People inquired about faith following some spiritual experience.

Preparation for Baptism

- Catechesis could begin with a formal request.

- The community may have given testimony about a candidate.

- Those seeking baptism were to turn away from their former beliefs.

- Preaching stressed the lordship of Christ.

- Belief in Jesus was to be manifest in one's behavior.

- Fasting and ritual prayer including handlaying may have preceded baptism.

- The length of prebaptismal catechesis remained brief.

Baptism

- Baptism in water affirmed belief in the name of Christ.

- Paul applied images of water, death and rising, oil and sealing, handlaying, clothing and light to explain baptism.

- Acts changes Saul's name to Paul following the baptism.

Life after Initiation

- After baptism Christians were to live as they believed.

4 ◆ Didache
Liturgy and Law

When the scribe finished his work he signed and dated the manuscript: Leo, 1056. Then he forgot about it. So did everyone else. Over eight hundred years later, in 1873, Archbishop Philotheos Bryennios, metropolitan of Nicomedia, discovered Leo's work in the library of the patriarch of Jerusalem at Constantinople. In 1883 he published what the scribe had copied by hand, a document called *Didache,* or *The Teaching of the Twelve Apostles.* It explained how to teach unbelievers, how to baptize and celebrate eucharist, and how to maintain church order while waiting for the coming of Christ. It claimed to be written by the twelve apostles. Most scholars reject this far-fetched allegation, but they do believe that what Bryennios found was a good copy of the first Christian handbook of catechesis, liturgy and law, a short but organized document assembled by the end of the first century in Syria or possibly Egypt.

Photo © Ross Burns

Roman theater at Bosra, Syria, second century.

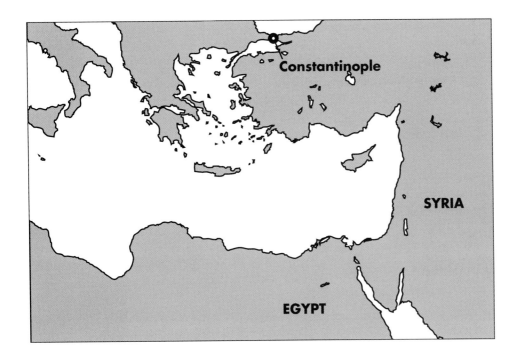

PREPARATION FOR BAPTISM

The *Didache* opens solemnly: "There are two ways, one of life and one of death." It then exhorts the reader to the way of life. This opening section may have served as a catechetical manual for those seeking baptism. Participation in the eucharist required baptism, and baptism required a proper disposition. In the section on the eucharist, the *Didache* becomes the first of many baptismal documents to quote Jesus' saying, "Do not give what is holy to dogs."

The document urges baptism in the name of the Trinity, in running water, after a fast, but it permits exceptions. The fast, lasting one or two days, applied not only to those to be baptized, but also to the minister and members of the community.

BAPTISM

The first word of this section, "Baptize," is plural, as in "All of you, baptize." The remaining instructions are singular. Perhaps more people than the leaders of the church administered baptism at this time. In the household of Cornelius, Peter had asked others to baptize (Acts 10:48). Paul had spoken of individuals who shared the ministry of baptism (1 Corinthians 1:12–16). But Ignatius of Antioch (+ c. 107) wrote, "It is not permitted

Baptize in running water, into the name of the Father and the Son and the Holy Spirit. If you do not have running water, baptize in some other water. If you cannot baptize in cold water, then use warm. If you do not have either, then pour water on the head three times, into the name of the Father and of the Son and of the Holy Spirit. Before the baptism, the one baptizing, the one being baptized, and all others who can should fast. You should exhort the baptized to fast for one or two days. . . .

But let no one eat or drink from your eucharist except those baptized into the name of the Lord. For the Lord said concerning this, "Do not give what is holy to dogs" (Matthew 7:6). *Didache 7, 9.*

to baptize without the bishop" (*Letter to the Smyrneans* 8:2). The *Didache* was not so restrictive.

Although the trinitarian formula for baptism appears in the *Didache* as it does in Matthew's gospel, the *Didache* also uses an alternate expression from Acts: It reserves the eucharist to those baptized in "the name of the Lord." This double attestation indicates that the formula of words for baptizing was still not universal.

The document clearly prefers baptism by immersion in a natural body of water. Not every community had access to running water, however, so alternatives were permitted. The peculiar preference for cold over warm water may favor natural sources over indoor containers. If all else failed, one could pour water over the candidate's head three times. This is the first explicit reference to baptism by pouring, although the New Testament does not exclude the possibility of this practice.

LIFE AFTER INITIATION

Baptism was essential for participation in the eucharist. The text does not explicitly state, however, that baptism took place in the context of eucharist.

◆◆◆

The *Didache* offers some information about the practice of baptism.

Preparation for Baptism

- Instruction centered on the "two ways," urging people to renounce one and accept the other.

- The person being baptized, the minister and the community fasted for one or two days.

Baptism

- Many people shared the ministry of baptizing.

- The formula for baptism was still stabilizing.

- Baptism by immersion three times in a natural water source was preferred.

- Baptism by pouring was permitted.

Life after Initiation

- The baptized could participate in the eucharist.

Justin ◆5
Apologist and Martyr

Justin was martyred by decapitation after he won an argument against the influential philosopher Crescens.

Over the years, Justin had become quite learned. Born a Gentile in Nablus, Samaria (c. 100), he studied the philosophies of his time, seeking truth among the Stoics, the Pythagoreans and the Platonists. He then learned the Christian philosophy and became more attracted to it after conversing with a stranger in a field.

© 2000 Passionist Research Center.

Blasphemous cross, Roman graffiti, second century.

All those who become convinced and believe that our teachings and doctrines are true, and who try to reform their life, learn from us how to pray and to fast, asking God for the forgiveness of their past sins. We join their prayer and their fast. Then they are brought by us to a place where there is water. There they are reborn in the manner of rebirth by which we ourselves were reborn. In the name of God the Father and Lord of the universe, and of our savior Jesus Christ, and of the Holy Spirit, they receive this bath in the water. . . . As for us, after the candidates have been washed, we lead those who have believed and confessed their faith to the place where the ones called "the brothers and sisters" have gathered.

. . . Now, we call this food "eucharist," and no one may take part of it except those who believe in the truth of our doctrines, who have been washed in the bath for the forgiveness of sins and rebirth, and who live life as Christ instructed.

First Apology 61:2–3; 65:1; 66:1

Struck by the logic of Christian thought, personal witness, a study of scripture and the amazing willingness of Christians to suffer martyrdom, Justin accepted baptism, probably at Ephesus. He established his own school in Rome. To confront prejudice and persecution, he wrote a defense of Christianity in two *Apologies* (meaning a defense or explanation) to the Roman emperor Antoninus Pius and his children, and to the senate and people of Rome.

The *First Apology* (c. 150) answered accusations against Christians and clarified what they do and do not believe. Then it more systematically treated the main points of Christian belief. Justin concluded the *First Apology* by describing baptism and eucharist.

Meanwhile, Justin continued debating Christianity with those who disagreed or did not understand. Crescens the Cynic, angry over losing a public disputation, had Justin arrested for being a Christian. Justin would not deny his faith at the trial. He accepted martyrdom in about the year 165. Six companions died with him, including a woman named Carito, a male slave named Euelpistus, and a bystander named Paeon, who was so impressed by the faith of the others that he volunteered the confession of his Christian belief. Some of Justin's remains are said to be interred in Rome at the Capuchin church of Santa Maria della Concezione, noted for its macabre collection of human bones.

FIRST INTEREST

Aspirants to Christianity in the second century expressed interest in the church due to various influences. In Justin's case, a combination of study, conversation and martyrs inspired him (*Dialogue with Trypho* 3–8). But Christianity probably spread best by word of mouth.

Justin implied that the catechist needed no special skill. One newly baptized woman tried to convince her intemperate husband to join her (*Second Apology* 2:2). The disabled and the blind, persons who knew neither alphabet nor grammar—all these taught the faith by common sense and personal witness. Human wisdom did not create Christian truths, Justin argued; the very power of God utters them (*First Apology* 60). Nonetheless, a skilled catechist proved beneficial: Persuasive arguments convinced budding philosophers. Justin's acceptance of Christianity demonstrated the power of cogent catechesis, and his *Apologies* relied on the assumption that conversion of heart would follow conviction of mind. A blend of

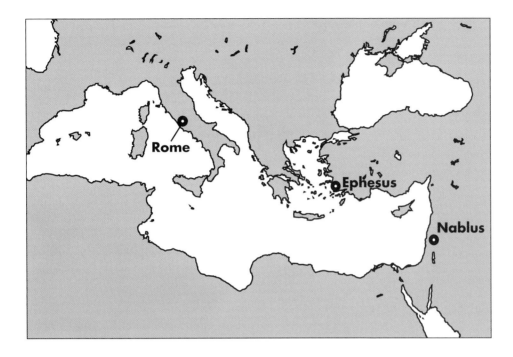

intellectual confidence and personal witness made outsiders curious about the Christian community.

PREPARATION FOR BAPTISM

Formation for baptism encompassed several techniques. Catechists handed on the teaching they received from the apostles. But these instructions were not simply intended to inform; their goal was to persuade, to convince, to invite belief and to cause those who heard them to reform their lives. Justin offered inquirers the same opportunity he had had for intellectual conversion—an understanding that leads to conviction. To assist the catechists, those seeking baptism and the entire community joined in the spiritual disciplines of fasting and prayer. Since baptism forgave sins, these activities helped people turn from their past as they embraced their new way of life. Justin does not indicate how long the preparation took, but it appears to have ranged from weeks to months. In any case, conversion depended on a blend of instruction, prayer, fasting, behavior and community life. This blend invited candidates to accept the way of Christ as it permitted the community to assess their sincerity

Any accessible location could serve as the place of instruction. Justin taught at home, an upstairs room in the house of a man named Martin, near the baths of Timothy (*Acts of Justin* 3:3).

BAPTISM

Justin called baptism regeneration and bath, metaphors suggesting a rebirth to a new way of life, and a cleansing from sin, surely administered by immersion. At the time of baptism the candidates were brought to the water, presumably by the members of the community. They went to "a place where there is water," probably a natural source, as the *Didache* preferred. There they were baptized in the name of the Trinity, a formula that Justin already regarded as traditional. He also speaks, though, of baptism "in the name of Jesus Christ . . . and in the name of the Holy Spirit" (*First Apology* 61), so the formula still lacked precision.

The baptized were then led to the place where the community had gathered for its great prayer of thanksgiving. This is the first explicit reference to the conferral of baptism within the context of eucharist. There prayers were offered for the assembly and for the baptized, for those "who had learned the truth" through their instruction, that they might live it accordingly. After the prayers they exchanged the community's kiss and received the body and blood of Christ.

When the newly baptized entered the community's life they were expected to have undergone a change from "necessity and ignorance" to "choice and knowledge." Justin calls baptism an "illumination," an entrance into a new state of mind.

◆◆◆

Justin, a product of intellectual conversion, dedicated his life to defending the Christian philosophy, and evoked from candidates for baptism an informed decision to reform their lives.

First Interest

• The death of martyrs drew attention to Christianity.

• Personal conversation with Christians provoked some to enter formation.

• The study of the scriptures and the Christian way of life gave Christianity a hearing within the schools of philosophy.

Preparation for Baptism

• Catechetical instruction was based on traditions attributed to the apostles.

• Preparation probably lasted up to several months in accessible places, such as homes.

• Instruction was intended to bring about an intellectual conviction.

• That conviction was to be evident in behavior.

• Prayer and fasting supported the instruction.

• The community joined in prayer and fasting.

• Those seeking baptism prepared for the forgiveness of sins.

Baptism

• Baptism took place at an outdoor water source.

• Some of the community brought those to be baptized to the water and then back to the assembly.

• Called "new birth" and "bath," baptism probably took place by immersion.

- The trinitarian formula for baptism was well known.

- Eucharist immediately followed baptism.

Life after Initiation

- The "illuminated" members of the community were expected to live in accordance with their conversion.

6 ◆ Clement of Alexandria
Philosopher and Tutor

Born about 150, probably at Athens, Clement anxiously sought far and wide for a teacher to quiet his inquisitive soul. He settled in Alexandria, Egypt, under the tutelage of Pantænus, the leader of the catechetical school there. He probably professed faith in Christ as an adult; afterward he had little patience for pagan religions, whose beliefs he considered devoid of value (see *The Exhortation to the Heathens*). Eventually he succeeded Pantænus as teacher. When the persecution of the Roman emperor Septimius Severus (202–203) darkened the shores of Egypt, Clement fled to Jerusalem and Antioch, and died in Cappadocia around the year 215.

Arch of Septimius Severus, Rome, second century.

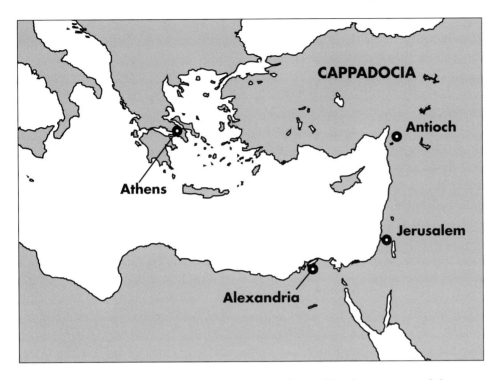

The works of Clement of Alexandria contain the earliest known use of the term *catechumen*. Although many people had undergone Christian catechesis prior to the second century, Clement gave his Egyptian followers a name that has endured. Still, the precise definition of the term as Clement used it remains unclear. He seems to use *catechumens* to mean the students in his school of Christian philosophy, who were expected to undergo a conversion but may not have been in immediate formation for baptism. Even so, by using terms like *catechumen, catechesis, catechetical* and even *catechumenal* for formation in Christ, Clement gave future generations a vocabulary for baptismal preparation.

The writings of Clement include *The Instructor,* in which he endorses temperate behavior while appealing to Christ the Instructor, and *Stromata,* or *The Miscellanies,* a collection of notes on Christian philosophy. These works placed Christianity in dialogue with contemporary philosophies and the experience of daily life.

Clement's work does not display Justin's interest in liturgy, nor does he dwell on the process of conversion. As a teacher he primarily taught Christians how to live their faith loyally. In doing so, he revealed his expectations of catechumens. None of his works systematically treats baptismal preparation.

By the end of the second century, baptismal preparation was slowly becoming institutionalized. Clement writes knowingly of different levels of formation. He uses the term *catechumens* in *The Instructor* (1:6) to speak about those who are still "children" in Christ, "newly catechized" but not "purified." Thus he distinguishes three groups: those who have been baptized, the unbaptized in catechetical formation and those outside the Christian family.

Let us consider the scripture, "I have not spoken to you as spiritual beings but as carnal beings, as children in Christ" (1 Corinthians 3:1). One may call "carnal" the new catechumens, still "children" in Christ. Paul calls "spiritual" those who already have faith in the Holy Spirit, even as he calls "carnal" the newly-catechized and not yet purified. Naturally he calls them "carnal" because they still have thoughts of the flesh as pagans do.

The Instructor 1:6

CATECHESIS

The content of the formation Clement offered centered on Christ, in imitation of the way the apostles formed new followers. Clement indicates that preaching Christ marked the early period of formation, then catechesis supported it. "'I have given you milk to drink and not solid food, for you are not yet able' (1 Corinthians 3:2). . . . If we understand the text in this way, we may say that milk is preaching poured out everywhere, and solid food is faith, firmly built into the form of a foundation by catechesis" (*The Instructor* 1:6). In *The Miscellanies* (5:10), he says catechetical instruction is milk, "the first food of the soul." He speaks of scriptural prophecy as the same kind of instruction received by "those who have become newly catechized," the catechumens (*The Miscellanies* 6:15).

PREPARATION FOR BAPTISM

Clement reports three years of "catechumenal instruction." Because the terminology was so new and so rare, however, "catechumenal instruction" in this case may not mean baptismal preparation; it more likely means a term in his catechetical school. He compares this instruction to the cultivation of trees in the Mosaic law (Leviticus 19:23–25).

According to Clement, newly planted trees need three years of nourishment (*The Miscellanies* 2:18). The caretaker removes any excess growth to keep the trees from being burdened and bent, weakened by the waste of nutrition. The caretaker will not pluck the fruit until the tree is mature, and the first fruit becomes an offering to God. In catechumenal instruction, Clement says, the teacher gives three years of care, cutting away the growth of sin until the fruit of faith has grown strong. Since he gives only this one temporal metaphor, it need not mean that baptismal preparation lasted three years. Nonetheless, in *The Instructor* (1:6) he acknowledges that "Catechesis leads progressively to faith. Faith, at the moment of baptism, receives the instruction of the Holy Spirit." Thus he expected prebaptismal catechesis to progress over time.

A ball game does not depend solely on the skill of the one who throws the ball, but on the rhythmic readiness of the catcher, so they can finish the game according to the rules. In the same way doctrine taught is suited to be believed.

The Miscellanies 2:6

Clement compares successful catechesis to a game of catch. The game relies not just on the skill of the pitcher, but also on the readiness of the catcher to join in the rhythm of the game. Similarly, catechesis depends not just on the instructor, but on those who will open their hearts to Christ. The comparison might apply to general catechetical formation, prebaptismal preparation, the Christian life after baptism, or to them all.

BAPTISM

Clement says very little about the liturgy of baptism. In *The Instructor* (1:6), he describes the effects of baptism: "We also, repenting of our sins, renouncing our iniquities, passing through the filter of baptism, flow back to the eternal light, children to the Father. . . . Baptized, we are illumined. Illumined, we are adopted as children. Adopted, we have been made perfect. Having been made perfect, we attain immortality." Since baptism required repentance and renunciation, it is possible that these were formal, independent parts of the ritual. Since baptism strained out what is bad, purified believers as through a filter and symbolized a new birth, it probably involved immersion.

◆◆◆

From the works of Clement of Alexandria, it can be seen that initiation was becoming more standardized.

Catechesis

- Participation in a Christian catechetical school could extend over three years.

- Those who participated were called *catechumens.*

Preparation for Baptism

- Preparation included preaching about Christ and catechetical formation.

- Catechumens were expected to repent and renounce their former behavior.

Baptism

- Baptism, probably by immersion, brought about purification and adoption.

7 ◆ Tertullian
Theologian and Ascetic

A woman whose name remains unknown convinced many North Africans that baptism was unnecessary and pointless. "Viper," Tertullian retorted, "viper that inhabits arid places." Little fish, the baptized, love the water, he continued. To plead his case, Tertullian wrote a treatise for those at risk, the first essay of this length on this topic. It is known by the simple title, *Baptism.*

Courtesy Opera di Religione, Diocesi of Ravenna.

Perpetua and Felicity, martyred in Carthage on March 7, 203, during the persecution of Septimius Severus. Catechumens when arrested, they accepted baptism shortly before their deaths.

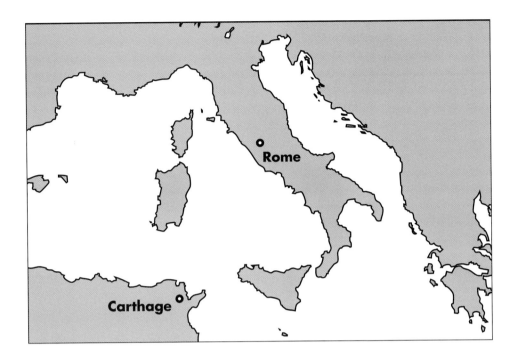

Carthage, a city in North Africa, had come under the rule of Rome, and Tertullian (c. 150–c. 220) probably spent time in both places. Born in Carthage probably of pagan parents, he may have been educated in Rome and may have served as a lawyer and a presbyter. A married man who probably was baptized as an adult, he became the first great theologian of the Latin language. He defended the orthodoxy of the church against heresies and persecutions. Early in the third century, however, Tertullian embraced the teachings of Montanism, a sect that awaited the immediate return of Christ and expected its adherents to follow a strict code of conduct supported by an ascetic spirituality. Some say he was drawn to it because the severity of the Montanist tenets appealed to his disciplined life; others say he fled to it because his quarrels with the Roman clergy got the best of his cantankerous temperament. Tertullian lived to be an old man and died after drifting from Montanism into a sect of his very own.

Even though *Baptism* advances Tertullian's most thorough exposition of initiation, his other works supply additional information. Together they offer a picture of baptismal preparation and celebration in early third-century Carthage.

Tertullian recognized different spiritual groups: pagans, catechumens and the faithful. (By this time the term *catechumen* had taken its more precise meaning, a person in baptismal formation.) Tertullian complained that heretics did not distinguish among these groups, who all gathered, learned and worshiped the same. Further, he charged, heretics even initiated catechumens before they were fully instructed (*Prescription against Heresies*, 41). Tertullian, echoing the *Didache* (9), advised Christians not to cast pearls before swine (*Baptism* 18; cf. Matthew 7:6): Pagans should not hear what catechumens heard; catechumens should not fully celebrate with the faithful.

CATECHESIS

If formation had a ceremonial beginning, it probably consisted of presenting one-self to a catechist, whom Tertullian called the "teacher or father of sacred matters" (*Apology* 8; *To the Nations* 1:7). Tertullian reveals nothing further about this; it may have entailed some ritual, or it may simply have involved showing up.

Readiness for baptism, according to Tertullian, depended on the circumstances, disposition and age of the candidate (*Baptism* 18). Even though Philip baptized the eunuch immediately (Acts of the Apostles 8:26–40) and Ananias baptized Paul after three days (Acts 9:11), Tertullian believed God treated them as special cases (*Baptism* 18). Preparation for the Christian's life, like preparation for the soldier's life, needed time (*Repentance* 6). Christians are made, he said, not born (*Apology* 18:4). In fact, Tertullian advised against baptizing children because they should first manifest better understanding and behavior (*Baptism* 18). Preparation in his community probably occupied up to several years.

> **Those about to enter baptism must pray with frequent prayers, fasts, time on their knees and all-night vigils. They must also confess all their past sins. . . . In this way we make up for past sins by mortifying our body and spirit, and build up defenses against temptations to come.**
>
> *Baptism* 20

But a lengthy baptismal preparation posed a problem. Some people began their formation, then showed no interest in finishing it. Learning that baptism would require a change in their behavior, some used their time of preparation not to correct their vices but to practice them (*Repentance* 6). Tertullian expected moral behavior, but he did not accept the extreme of the Marcionites, a heretical sect that disparaged the Old Testament and marriage, and required catechumens to be virgins, celibate, widowed, divorced or castrated (*Against Marcion* 1:29; 4:11; 4:34). Tertullian did not expect unmarried catechumens, only intentionally repentant ones.

PREPARATION FOR BAPTISM

As baptism drew near, catechumens made a special preparation. Although Tertullian recounts no specific rituals early in formation, several immediately preceded baptism. Still, he notes their great simplicity, performed without pretense (*Baptism* 2). He described these catechumens with new terminology: "those about to enter baptism" (*Baptism* 20) or "those going into the water" (*Repentance* 6:9).

BAPTISM

Tertullian preferred that baptism take place at the vigils of Easter and Pentecost, but he permitted it on any day (*Baptism* 19).The minister should be a bishop, but if he so delegated, a presbyter or deacon could baptize, or even a lay male.

Those about to enter the water met with the community to pray, fast, kneel, keep vigil, confess their sins and mortify their flesh and their spirit to protect themselves from future temptations (*Baptism* 20). This confession of sins probably included a formal renunciation of the devil: During the Montanist period of his life, Tertullian recalled that catechumens renounce the devil, his works and his angels before being baptized (*The Crown* 3).

Tertullian is the first source in the West to include a blessing of water in the rite of baptism (*Baptism* 4). Water in a sufficient but not overpowering quantity was used: Catechumens were dipped in water, but came up no cleaner physically (*Baptism* 2). The writer tolerated a variety of water sources: sea, pond, river, fountain, cistern or tub (*Baptism* 4).

Few words were used in the rite (*Baptism* 2), and he suggests that those to be baptized professed their belief by responding to questions, such as "Do you believe in God?" They professed belief not only in the Trinity but also in the church (*Baptism* 6; 13). Tertullian stated that the church seals one's faith with baptism, a faith in God the creator, in Jesus son of Mary, in the resurrection and in the scriptures, a faith that united the church of Africa with that of Rome (*Prescription against Heretics* 36).

Baptism is the first treatise to make an explicit reference to sponsors, but only in the case of little children (18): Dissuading the baptism of the young, Tertullian cautions that their sponsors may die before completing their responsibility. He also refers to the baptized being "raised up" or "taken up" from the font, which could imply that even adults had a sponsor: "We renounce the devil and his empty promises and his angels. We are immersed three times, responding somewhat more fully than our Lord has prescribed in the gospel. Having been raised up, we taste a mixture of milk and honey. From that day for a whole week we abstain from the daily bath" (*The Crown* 3). However, it is not clear whether some individuals embraced specific responsibilities or if sponsorship fell to the entire community.

Immediately after baptism several other procedures followed. The newly baptized were anointed with blessed oil, as Aaron was anointed a priest (Exodus 29:7; Leviticus 8:12) and as Jesus was anointed with the Spirit (Acts 4:27). Since Tertullian compares this physical anointing to a spiritual one, the oil may have covered the body: "Then having gone up from the bath we are anointed with a blessed anointing of ancient discipline, by which people were accustomed to be anointed for priesthood, by oil from a horn from which Aaron was anointed by Moses. . . . Next, calling and inviting the Holy Spirit, the hand is imposed in blessing" (*Baptism* 7:1; 8:1).

A signation may have occurred at this point, since Tertullian speaks of Christians having been signed with the cross (*The Prescription against Heresies* 40; *The Resurrection of the Flesh* 8; *Against Marcion* 3:22). Next he affirms that the newly baptized received an imposition of hands with a prayer invoking the Holy Spirit (*Baptism* 8; *The Resurrection of the Flesh* 8). Furthermore, he exhorts the newly baptized to pray with the community when they come up from the font (*Baptism* 20). In Montanist works, Tertullian says they then drink a mixture of milk and honey (*Against Marcion* 1:14; *The Crown* 3), which may have accompanied the eucharist, but he does not say so explicitly in *Baptism.* Tertullian permitted the prebaptismal fast to continue even after baptism, in imitation of Jesus' postbaptismal fast in the desert, but he did not endorse it (*Baptism* 20).

◆◆◆

In third-century Carthage, the catechumenate and baptism assumed more definition.

Catechesis

- To begin preparation candidates presented themselves to a catechist.

- Formation could take some years to complete.

- It called for sincere repentance.

Preparation for Baptism

- Catechumens were called "those about to enter the water."

Baptism

- Prayer, fasting, confession of sins and renunciation of the devil in the presence of the community all preceded baptism.

- Easter and Pentecost became preferred occasions for baptism, but any day was permitted.

- The bishop was the preferred minister, but he could delegate to a presbyter, deacon or a lay male.

- Water from a natural or collected source was blessed.

- Those to be baptized made a profession of faith in the Trinity and in the church.

- Baptism was by immersion.

- Sponsors stood ready to assist.

- The newly baptized were anointed with blessed oil.

- Their foreheads were signed with a cross.

- They received an imposition of hands and a prayer for the Holy Spirit.

- They may have received the bread and wine of the eucharist with a mixture of milk and honey.

Life after Initiation

- The baptized continued some spiritual disciplines.

Origen ◆8
Student and Teacher

By the age of eighteen Origen (c. 185–253) held a job as teacher at the catechetical school in Alexandria from which his own instructor, Clement, had fled during the persecution of the emperor Septimius Severus. The same persecution had claimed the life of Origen's father, making him, the eldest child of a large Christian family, head of the household. He would have followed his father into martyrdom, but his mother hid his clothes. The local bishop, Demetrius, appointed him head of the Egyptian school at which Christians, pagans and heretics enrolled to learn the Christian philosophy or to prepare for baptism.

Christ and Saint Menas. Menas was a Roman soldier who refused to renounce Christ. He was martyred near Alexandria in 296.

According to some, Origen's brilliant mind did not temper his eccentric asceticism. During his travels his oratorical skills so impressed his hearers that another bishop ordained him a presbyter. Demetrius disputed the ordination on the grounds that Origen had castrated himself. Demetrius expelled the great teacher from Alexandria about 231.

Origen settled at Caesarea in Palestine, where he served as presbyter and wrote many of his works on Christian philosophy and biblical studies. Although none of these systematically treated baptismal preparation and celebration, he frequently referred to the practice he knew either from Alexandria or Caesarea. When Decius seized power as emperor in 249 he authorized a full persecution of Christians throughout the empire. Origen was arrested and tortured; he died at Tyre in the year 253.

Not all of Origen's students became Christians. As in other schools of philosophy, some attended out of curiosity or a desire for learning; others came to adopt the promoted way of life. Origen called them all "hearers," whether or not they were preparing for baptism (see *Homily 12 on Jeremiah* 3).

FIRST INTEREST

People investigated Christianity either because of the influence of the school (*Against Celsus* 3:51) of Christian families (*Against Celsus* 3:55) or of the example of martyrs and confessors (*Homily 4 on Jeremiah* 3). Some Christians actually traveled through cities, towns and remote dwellings to seek converts (*Against Celsus* 3:9).

At the beginning, when you decided to become catechumens, you might well have been told, "Choose this day whom you will serve" (Joshua 24:15). . . . Now it is out of place to speak to you in that way. . . . In the promises you once made concerning the worship of God, you gave this reply to the catechists: "We too will serve the Lord, for he is our God" (Joshua 24:18).

Exhortation to Martyrdom 17

When hearers of the Christian philosophy sought to become Christians, they formed a separate group (*Against Celsus* 3:51). Those who believed anti-Christian propaganda learned about good and evil within the context of an orderly universe, and about the creator responsible for it all (*Against Celsus* 8:52). These were invited to abandon their false idols (*Against Celsus* 3:15).

CATECHESIS

Within that group of aspirants Origen distinguished a further group, those making immediate preparation for baptism. Teachers asked them to abandon their false gods and serve the Christian God, marking a rite of entrance to catechumenal formation (*Exhortation to Martyrdom* 17). Because of their virtuous life, these helped judge the sincerity of future candidates (*Against Celsus* 3:51).

Origen made a firm distinction between catechumens and faithful (see, for instance, *Homilies on Jeremiah* 4:3, 14:4 and 18:8) and compared the time in formation to Israel's progress in the desert. Catechumens abandoned idolatry and accepted the commandments of the church; thus they "crossed the Red Sea" in their desire to hear God's law each day.

Just as Israel crossed the Jordan into the promised land, so would the catechumens complete their journey with baptism (*Homily on Joshua* 4:1). When the Israelites left Egypt, their diets developed in three stages: the food they packed for departure, the manna in the desert and the vegetation of the promised land. Those preparing for baptism ate the simple food of generic instruction, then the "desert food" of God's law during the catechumenate and finally the rich food of the Christian passover (*Homily on Joshua* 6:1).

Origen knew of the more common tradition connecting baptism with the crossing not of the Jordan but of the Red Sea (see *Homily 5 on Exodus* 1), but by speaking of baptism in terms of the Jordan he was able to make parallels with the cleansing of Naaman and the baptism of Jesus, calling candidates to conversion and belief by means of commentary on the scriptures (*Commentary on John* 6:220, 242).

> **Christians as far as possible first test the souls of those who want to become their hearers, having instructed them in private. When they appear sufficiently to have the desire for a virtuous life, and not before, Christians introduce them to the community. They form a separate group of those who are beginners and are receiving admission, but who have not yet received the sign of complete purification.**
>
> **Another group is formed of those who have shown to the best of their ability their intention to desire nothing but what Christians approve. Among these, certain ones are appointed to inquire about the lives and behavior of the candidates, to keep access to the public assembly from those guilty of secret sins, but to welcome others with their whole heart, to make them better each day.** *Against Celsus* 3:51

PREPARATION FOR BAPTISM

The period of preparation for baptism included doctrinal and moral formation. Catechumens learned about the Christian precepts of faith, including the Trinity, eternal life, human freedom and the scriptures (*Principles* Preface 2). Since baptism would offer forgiveness of sins, Origen recommended making its preparation a time of repentance (*Homily 21 on Luke* 4).

Some leaders in the community performed exorcisms. In one place, Origen says, "The faithful teachers put to flight numberless demons, that they may no longer fool souls by their trickery" (*Homily 16 on Leviticus* 7). It is not clear, however, if those who were exorcised were people in baptismal formation or those learning about Christianity in general. Other exorcisms (see, for example, *Against Celsus* 1:6 and 25) pertained to spiritual and physical well-being, and consisted of the proclamation of the gospel and of the name of Jesus.

Origen does not specify the length of time that a catechumen spent in preparation. He comments (*Homily 6 on John* 144–145) on the three years required for a tree to bear good fruit in Leviticus (19:23–25), as his predecessor Clement had done, but once again he was probably referring to the catechetical school, not to baptismal preparation.

> **When those who have been turned toward virtue have made progress and shown that they have been purified by the word and have led a better life as far as they can, then and not before do we invite them to participation in our mysteries.**
>
> *Against Celsus* 3:59

The community issued an invitation to baptism to those who had progressed in a virtuous life (*Against Celsus* 3:59). Those who delayed their responses were urged to present themselves soon. "Catechumens, do not remain catechumens a long time, but hurry to receive the grace of God that you may be numbered among the gathering of the children of Israel" (*Homily 9 on Joshua* 9). Origen says no more about how that invitation to baptism was extended.

BAPTISM

Origen reports the basics about the baptismal ritual: the use of water and the invocation of the Trinity (see, for example, *Principles* 1:3, 2). Nowhere does he recommend a time of year, so it is unknown if he celebrated baptisms at Easter. He frowned on blessing water, since water already had the property of imparting purity (*Fragments on John* 3:3). A renunciation of former ways preceded baptism: "When we come to the grace of baptism, renouncing all other gods and rulers, we confess the only God, Father, Son and Holy Spirit" (*Homily 8 on Exodus* 4).

In several passages Origen indicates that an anointing with chrism accompanied baptism (for example, *Homily 6 on Leviticus* 5; *Homily 9 on Leviticus* 9; *Homily 7 on Ezekiel* 4), but it is not clear if he is referring to a prebaptismal or postbaptismal anointing.

Regarding other rituals, such as giving a white garment or participating in the eucharist, Origen only speaks in allegorical terms, so it is not clear if these elements were part of the baptismal rite. "You cannot hear the word of God unless you have washed your garments. For a little later you shall go in to the wedding dinner, you shall eat from the flesh of the lamb and drink the cup of salvation" (*Homily 11 on Exodus* 7).

◆◆◆

Origen was familiar with many elements of a catechumenate and baptism.

First Interest

- Christianity attracted people because of the witness of families, the influence of the schools and the example of martyrs.

- Those in the Christian school who wanted to adopt this way of life began to learn its basics.

Catechesis

- Entrance into catechesis required a ritual renunciation of idols.

- Those aspiring to the Christian life learned about good and evil, and the creator of all.

Preparation for Baptism

- Teachers invited conversion and belief by commenting on the scriptures.

- Instruction included doctrinal and moral formation.

- Exorcisms may have been part of this period.

- The length of formation cannot be determined, nor the occasion for baptism.

- The community issued an invitation to baptism to those who were prepared.

Baptism

- Water was not blessed.

- Candidates for baptism renounced Satan and confessed their allegiance to God.

- People were baptized in water in the name of the Trinity.

- Candidates were anointed with blessed oil either before or after baptism.

9 ◆ Apostolic Tradition
Organization and Compilation

In 1848, an ancient manuscript written in the Bohairic dialect of Coptic was discovered. Early in the twentieth century, several scholars concurred that it was a translation of the *Apostolic Tradition*, first composed in Greek by Hippolytus around 215. Large and small parts of it turned up in other languages in Syria, North Africa and Italy, suggesting that the work enjoyed wide circulation. Its depiction of initiation seemed to fill out the scant information from early third-century sources. The *Apostolic Tradition* came to be regarded as the single most influential document in the history of the catechumenate.

Statue of Hippolytus.

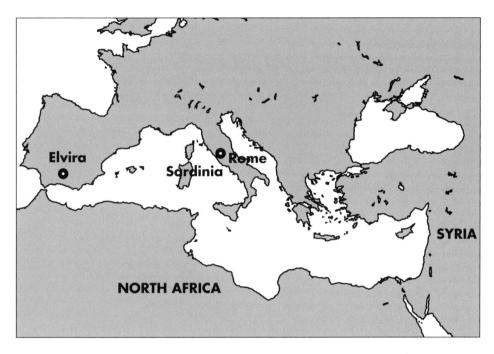

Late in the twentieth century, however, scholars disputed the date of the work, its authorship and even its authority. The work seems to have been compiled from several sources over the span of a century. Its author may have rendered his own experience of initiation, may have reported his knowledge of more ancient observances, or may even have written what he hoped initiation would look like. So what appeared to be true—that in this document Hippolytus wrote a description of the early third-century baptismal rites in Rome—is probably not the case.

A list of the works of Hippolytus, made long after his death, included one titled the *Apostolic Tradition*, but the list's accuracy is now disputed. Besides, the earliest versions of what is now called the *Apostolic Tradition* carry neither that title nor an attribution to Hippolytus. That work is likely a collection of texts from Rome and other liturgical centers compiled between the early third and the mid-fourth century. Even though its authorship is disputed and its title is questionable, the work called the *Apostolic Tradition* still has great value in the history of the catechumenate.

Hippolytus (c. 170–c. 235) was a writer, an embittered presbyter, a schismatic, an antipope, a martyr and a saint. He despised an old acquaintance, Callistus, who became the deacon of Pope Zephyrinus. Hippolytus criticized the pope's theology, grew completely surly when Callistus acceded to Peter's chair, declared himself a bishop, drew a minuscule following and ended up suffering in the persecution of Emperor Maximinus I. As an old man he was sentenced to hard labor, probably at Sardinia, and died there with Pope Pontian, with whom he must have reached some reconciliation. They share a feast day, August 13, on which Hippolytus is remembered as a martyr and presbyter, not as a bishop.

The writer of the *Apostolic Tradition*, who was probably not this Hippolytus, intended to present the tradition of the church, purportedly as handed down from the apostles. He hoped that its readers would then keep that tradition more strongly. Not an innovator, he must have observed some dissent from the tradition and hoped to stop it.

The work has three parts. It opens with an essay on church structure, including texts for the ordinations of a bishop, a presbyter and a deacon; prayers for the appointment of confessors, widows and readers; and rules governing virgins, subdeacons and healers. Its example of the eucharistic prayer for the ordination of a bishop ultimately became the model for Eucharist Prayer II in the twentieth-century Roman Catholic church. The work concludes with notices on a variety of observances, including fasting, eating, drinking, care for the sick and prayer for different times of the day. The middle part extensively presents catechumenal and baptismal rites.

The *Apostolic Tradition* offers the earliest comprehensive look at a catechumenate in stages and an elaborate rite of initiation.

CATECHESIS

To begin (*Apostolic Tradition* 15), those who wanted to "hear the word" were brought by someone in the community to teachers at the place where the community would gather to hear the scriptures. The teachers, who could be clergy or laity, opened an inquiry on the newcomers to examine their motives, their marital status, civil status (slave or free) and profession. Those excluded from formation (16) included traffickers in prostitution; soldiers who kill; priests of idolatry and makers of idols; entertainers such as actors, magicians, charioteers, gladiators; and producers of such shows. Someone from the community, a kind of sponsor, would give testimony to help the teachers discern the motives of those who came, their freedom to join and their capacity for instruction.

Catechumens spent three years in formation (17), but this period was shortened for those with outstanding behavior. The length of formation recalls the three-year periods of study mentioned in the works of Clement and Origen in Alexandria. If terms at philosophical schools were lasting this long, Christian formation may have copied this custom. Even though the *Apostolic Tradition* called for a three-year formation, other evidence indicates that this was not widely implemented. During this period, the length of formation was adapted to individual circumstances. By the early fourth century, for example, the Council of Elvira in Spain recommended a catechumenate of two years (42), which could be lengthened to three (4) or five (73) years, or even to the end of one's life (68), depending on one's behavior. The *Recognitions* of Pseudo-Clement (3:67), a work that probably originated in early third-century Syria, recommended a three-month preparation for baptism.

During the period of formation, each gathering of catechumens began with instruction and prayer (18). Then the catechumens joined the rest of the community, where the women, their heads covered, stood apart from the men. Catechumens were not to exchange the kiss of peace, a sign of membership in the Christian community. After the prayer, the teacher imposed hands and dismissed the catechumens (19).

The imposition of hands that closed the catechumens' prayer during this period resembles a gesture already seen in the scriptures: Ananias placed his hands on Saul shortly before his baptism (Acts 9:17–18; 22:12–16), and Jesus often touched those whom he cured (see, for example, Mark 7:31–37).

During this lengthy period of preparation, any catechumens who suffered martyrdom before baptism were considered baptized by their own blood. That such a statement exists in this document soberly recollects what people risked for their faith in Christ. By the witness of martyred catechumens and the perseverance of the faithful, Christianity eventually gained political tolerance. The absence of need for such statements in later catechumenal texts came at a great price.

PREPARATION FOR BAPTISM

Several actions took place just before baptism (20). Catechumens were examined again, this time to investigate not just their background, but also their behavior. Did they live piously, honor widows, visit the sick, and perform other good deeds?

This second examination intensified the first. Its appearance echoes the story of Cornelius (Acts 10), whose desire for baptism was twice reported to Peter. The investigation centered on behavior, not on participation at the instructions or on understanding them. This emphasis may indicate that the ones leading the examination were the teachers, the same ones who had performed the first inquiry. They would already know about participation and understanding, but would need testimony from the community about the way the catechumens lived. Presumably, catechumens would have devoted some time to interacting with those who would ultimately bear witness on their behalf.

> **When these three months are over you may be baptized on the feast day. Each of you will be baptized in running water in the name of the Threefold Beatitude invoked upon you, having first been anointed with oil sanctified by prayer, so that consecrated by these things you may finally receive from what is holy.**
>
> Pseudo-Clement, *Recognitions* 3:67

If they passed the examination, they were invited to "hear the gospel." This expression implies that catechumens had thus far been dismissed from the assembly prior to its proclamation. At this point, the catechumens were called "the chosen who are set apart to receive baptism," suggesting that some discussion of their election must have taken place.

After the examination, preparation for baptism continued with daily hand-layings and exorcisms (20). The exorcisms helped the community to discern the presence of faith. Since faith is God's gift, the faithful searched the catechumens for its presence at prayer. When the bishop breathed on the chosen ones, he ritualized the community's prayer that the Holy Spirit replace the exorcised spirit. The forehead, ears, and nose were signed, probably with a cross. This procedure calls to mind two biblical events: God breathing into the nostrils of the newly created human (Genesis 2:7), signifying that God will recreate people through baptism; and Jesus' exorcism of a man who was blind and mute (Matthew 12:22–29). This miracle has a parallel in Mark (3:22–27). In Luke's version (11:14–28) Jesus implies he casts out demons by "the finger of God," an expression that may have inspired the signation at this exorcism.

If the exorcisms revealed that some catechumens were not purified, their baptism was delayed; so also was the baptism of women who were menstruating.

BAPTISM

In this section, the *Apostolic Tradition* never specifically mentions the time of year. Tertullian preferred Easter and Pentecost for baptism, but this work, like Origen, never states a preference. Baptism may have happened more than once a year to accommodate those who were deferred.

On Thursday those to be baptized bathed; they fasted on Friday and Saturday. These fast days recall the practices of Saul, the *Didache* and Justin. During the day on Saturday, the bishop conducted the handlaying and exorcism; while they knelt he breathed on them, "sealed" or signed each one's forehead, ears and nose, and then he raised them up. They brought an offering for the eucharist that evening. They spent all night in vigil, reading the scriptures and receiving instruction.

Baptism followed (21). After the all-night vigil, at cockcrow, the deacons and presbyters led the chosen ones to a water source apart from the community, where they prayed over the water. Meanwhile, the bishop, still with the assembly, blessed an oil of exorcism and another of thanksgiving. At the water, separating into groups of men, women and children, the chosen removed their clothes. Women loosened their hair and removed all jewelry so no profane object accompanied them into the blessed water.

Beginning with the children, then the men, and then the women, the presbyter held each one and asked them to make the statement, "I renounce you, Satan, and all your empty promises and all your works." (If the children seeking baptism were very young, their parents or another family member answered for them.) A deacon arrived, carrying the blessed oils from the bishop. The presbyter anointed the chosen one with the oil of exorcism, saying, "Let every evil spirit depart far from you." He entered the water, and a deacon walked with the naked supplicant toward him.

The presbyter placed a hand on the chosen one and asked, "Do you believe in one God the Father almighty?"

"I believe," came the response.

The presbyter baptized him or her once in the water. "Do you believe in Christ Jesus, the Son of God, who was born of the Holy Spirit and the Virgin Mary, was crucified under Pontius Pilate, died, rose alive from the dead on the third day, ascended into heaven, sits at the right hand of the Father, and will come to judge the living and the dead?"

"I believe."

He baptized a second time. "Do you believe in the Holy Spirit in the holy church and the resurrection of the flesh?"

"I believe."

The presbyter baptized a third time. Interspersing the action of baptism with the profession of faith communicated a dramatic unity between baptism and faith.

The presbyter anointed each one coming up from the water with the oil of thanksgiving. "I anoint you with holy oil in the name of Jesus Christ." All who were baptized dried themselves, put on their clothes and took their places with the assembly and the bishop.

The *Apostolic Tradition* describes two anointings, one before baptism and one after. Tertullian had reported only the one following baptism. By the third century, several Syrian sources (for example, a Syriac edition of the *Didascalia*, the *Recognitions* of Pseudo-Clement, the *Acts of Judas Thomas* and the *History of John, Son of Zebedee*) indicated only one anointing, but it preceded baptism. Because the sequence of baptismal rites varied in different parts of the Christian world at this time, it is not known for certain if the *Apostolic Tradition* really knew an old tradition of two anointings, or if it struck a compromise between the two practices by incorporating them both. To its credit, this source distinguishes the purposes of the anointings much more clearly than its contemporaries. The distinction of ministries throughout this section is also noteworthy.

After the newly baptized joined the assembly, several other rites followed (21). The bishop extended his hand and prayed that those reborn of the Holy Spirit might receive God's grace. Then he poured the oil of thanksgiving and laid his hand on the head of each, saying, "I anoint you with holy oil in God the Father almighty and Christ Jesus and the Holy Spirit." He "sealed" each one's forehead (probably with a cross) and gave the Christian kiss. "The Lord be with you," he said. "And also with you," each replied.

The eucharist followed; the bishop exhorted the newly baptized with an explanation of its meaning. At communion the bishop distributed the bread of the eucharist. Presbyters or deacons offered a series of cups: first of water, for an interior washing to imitate the exterior baptism; then of milk and honey, recalling the land promised their ancestors (Leviticus 20:24); and finally the cup of wine of the eucharist. "In God the Father almighty," each minister said. "Amen," the communicant replied each time. "And in the Lord Jesus Christ and in the Holy Spirit and the holy church," he continued. "Amen."

The postbaptismal rituals in this document are more elaborate than what Tertullian described. Noteworthy is the bishop's prayer for God's grace, accompanied by an imposition of hands and an anointing with oil. The expressive multistation communion rite with its explanatory exhortation concluded a striking celebration.

LIFE AFTER INITIATION

After these rituals, the *Apostolic Tradition* encouraged all to be zealous in good works and to please God by putting into practice what they had learned (21). If the baptized needed further instruction about what they had experienced, the bishop became their teacher, and he explained these matters to them in secret. This instruction, which appears only in the late manuscripts of the *Apostolic Tradition*, is the earliest example of mystagogy, a post-initiatory catechesis.

◆◆◆

During the third century the initiation rites became much more elaborate.

Catechesis

- Someone from the community presented candidates to teachers at the place where the faithful gathered.

- Teachers conducted a basic inquiry into the candidates' background.

- The catechumenate may have lasted up to three years, but the time was adaptable.

- Sessions included scripture, prayer and handlaying.

- Catechumens were expected to have contact with other members of the community.

- They performed a variety of good works.

Preparation for Baptism

- Those preparing for baptism were recognized as "chosen."

- They underwent another examination, this time into their behavior.

- Every day they experienced handlaying and exorcisms.

- They bathed on the Thursday before baptism and fasted on Friday and Saturday.

- The bishop conducted the Saturday exorcism, during which he breathed on those to be baptized and "sealed" each one's forehead, nose and eyes.

- Those to be baptized spent the night hearing the scriptures and receiving instruction.

Baptism

- The document stressed no single time of year for baptisms.

- Presbyters and deacons led those to be baptized to a water source apart from the community.

- They blessed the water.

- Those to be baptized removed their clothes, renounced Satan, and received an anointing of exorcism from the presbyter.

- They entered the water, professed their faith in the Trinity, and were immersed three times.

- They were anointed with the oil of thanksgiving by the bishop, and put on their clothes.

- Joining the assembly, they received handlaying from the bishop, who said a prayer for God's grace, anointed them and kissed them.

- The bishop exhorted the newly baptized at communion.

- At communion the newly baptized received bread, water, a mixture of milk and honey, and wine.

Life after Initiation

- The bishop explained the meaning of the initiation rites in secret.

- The newly baptized put into practice what they had learned.

10 ✦ Apostolic Constitutions
Origins and Variations

The role of women in church leadership needed attention in late fourth-century Syria, as it had in previous years. A document that prohibited women to baptize but permitted them to serve as deaconesses during baptism was published around 380, probably in Antioch. Under the title *Apostolic Constitutions*, the work purported to be a collection of decrees handed down from the apostles, but it actually was compiled, edited and adapted from several previous publications. These included the *Didache*, the *Apostolic Tradition* and the work that had already taken up the question of deaconesses, the *Didascalia*, which probably first appeared in Syria in the first half of the third century. In eight chapters the *Apostolic Constitutions* treats topics including Christian behavior, church hierarchy and baptism.

Yale University Art Gallery, Dura-Europos Collection.

Reconstructed font in the baptistry of the house church at Dura-Europos, Syria, c. 240.

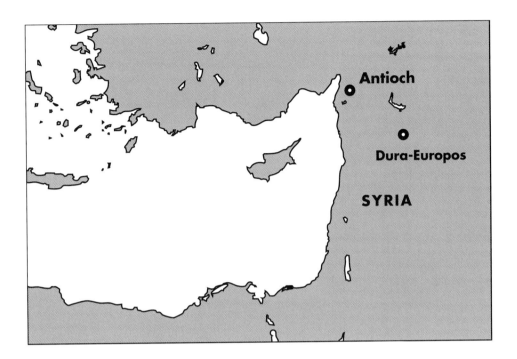

The *Apostolic Constitutions* went through several editors and the resulting work shows not unity but variety, if not internal disagreement. At least four of its sources handled the topics of catechumens or baptism, so the *Apostolic Constitutions* reported what they had written, with some adaptations, without attempting a synthesis.

In a passage lifted directly from the *Didascalia,* those seeking baptism first had to convert from their former way of life. Their repentance entitled them to "hear the word" in church; after baptism they shared communion (2:38–39).

Initiation must have required a discernment by leaders of the community based on some kind of testimony or observation, but the document never reports its content and extent.

The *Apostolic Constitutions* illuminates this text in another section adapted from the *Didascalia,* on the services of widows, deaconesses and deacons. It reserved the ministry of baptism to bishops (3:9–11) and recommended the assistance of deacons and deaconesses in its administration (3:15–18). Deacons anointed the forehead of all the candidates; then deaconesses anointed the women's bodies, and deacons the men's. The bishop imposed hands and anointed the head. The bishop or presbyter then baptized, and deacons and deaconesses received the newly baptized from the font. The bishop anointed them again. The baptized were to live free from sin, having renounced Satan and prayed the Lord's Prayer.

When unbelievers wish to repent we bring them into the church to hear the word, but we do not have communion with them until they have received the seal of baptism.

Apostolic Constitutions 2:39

In the latter part of the *Apostolic Constitutions* a brief baptismal ritual inspired by a second source, the *Didache,* appears (7:22). Those preparing for baptism were expected to fast. The bishop anointed them, baptized them with water and sealed them again with oil. These anointings were not essential; water baptism sufficed. "You, bishop, shall first anoint them with holy oil, and then baptize them with

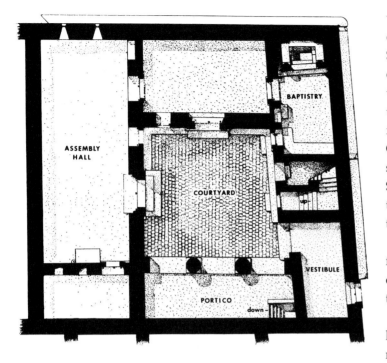

Yale University Art Gallery, Dura-Europos Archive.

Plan of the Christian building, Dura-Europos, Syria, c. 240.

water, and finally seal them with oil, that the oil may be a participation with the Holy Spirit, the water a symbol of death, and the ointment the seal of the covenants. But if there is no oil or ointment, water suffices for the anointing, for the seal, and for the confession of the one dying, or dying with Christ. Before baptism, those to be baptized should fast" (*Apostolic Constitutions* 7:22). Sections about fasting, the Lord's Prayer, and the eucharist follow, but it is not clear that they pertain to baptism.

A third presentation of baptism comes from an unknown source (7:39–45). It describes both prebaptismal instruction and the ritual.

During their instruction, catechumens learned (39) about creation, God's punishment of the wicked and glorification of the good, while a minister offered handlaying and prayer for purification. Catechumens then learned about the mysteries of the life of Jesus. The length of preparation is not specified, but the time seems focused rather than prolonged.

The baptismal rites (40) were not associated with any time of the liturgical year. Catechumens prepared to renounce the devil and join Christ. They underwent a moral conversion, which purified their hearts of evil. As a result, catechumens made a statement renouncing Satan, his works and empty promises, and associated themselves with Christ, expressing their belief in the Trinity (41). The

In the baptism of women, the deacon shall anoint only their forehead with the holy oil, and after him the deaconess shall anoint them. It is not necessary that women should be seen by men. You, bishop, should anoint her head only in handlaying.

. . . Either you, bishop, or a presbyter under you, should in the solemn form name over them the Father, Son, and Holy Spirit, and baptize them in the water. Let a deacon receive the man and a deaconess the woman. In this way this inviolable seal may happen with appropriate decorum. After that, bishop, anoint those that are baptized with oil.

Apostolic Constitutions 3:16

bishop blessed oil (42) for the forgiveness of sins and anointed the catechumens in preparation for baptism. He then blessed water and baptized in the name of the Trinity. He blessed another oil and, after laying hands on them, he anointed the newly baptized. Afterward, they prayed the Lord's Prayer, standing and facing east. This ritual makes no specific mention of eucharist.

In the final section the *Apostolic Constitutions* considers catechumens (8:32), based on information excerpted from the *Apostolic Tradition*.

Those seeking baptism were first brought by deacons to the bishop or presbyters, and their motives were examined. The deacons gave testimony based on what they had learned from others. "Those who first come to the mystery of blessedness should be brought to the bishop or to the presbyters by the deacons, and asked why they should be admitted to the word of the Lord. Those who bring them offer testimony about them, carefully investigating the things they observe" (*Apostolic Constitutions* 8:32). The list of suspicious professions had grown from that in the *Apostolic Tradition*. The length of formation was specified at three years, but its abridgment was permitted for the diligent.

This final section of the *Apostolic Constitutions* describes prayers for catechumens, including an imposition of hands and a dismissal from worship (8:6; 8:8; 8:12; 8:35), though they are not drawn from the *Apostolic Tradition*.

Differences from the *Apostolic Tradition* emerge: Originally, members of the community presented those seeking baptism to teachers; here, deacons present them to the clergy. The deacons do not even know those inquiring, since they must ask others about their worthiness. This excerpt remains silent about exorcisms and the second examination before baptism. It does not go on to treat baptism.

◆◆◆

Although these sections all appear in the same late fourth-century work, they do not offer a consistent vision of preparation for catechumens. Some conclusions may still be drawn.

Catechesis

- In one tradition deacons inquired about the character of potential catechumens and presented them to the bishop and presbyters, who examined their way of life.

- In another tradition those who repented were accepted into formation.

- One source recommended a three-year formation, but other evidence suggests it was briefer.

Preparation for Baptism

- Catechumens were welcomed to a word service, then prayers were offered for them and they were dismissed.

- Catechumens were expected to undergo an interior, moral conversion, turning from sin.

- One source indicates that catechesis included topics such as creation, morality and Jesus Christ, accompanied by an imposition of hands for the forgiveness of sins in preparation for baptism.

- Catechumens fasted before baptism.

Baptism

- No specific occasion for baptism was suggested.

- Those to be baptized renounced Satan.

- According to one witness, the deacon anointed the foreheads of candidates with blessed oil. Deacons and deaconesses assisted in anointing the bodies of catechumens. The bishop gave an anointing and imposed hands before baptism.

- After a profession of faith, the naked candidates received baptism in the name of the Trinity.

- Deacons and deaconesses assisted those coming up from the font.

- The baptized received another anointing with an imposition of hands.

- The recitation of the Lord's Prayer followed, and perhaps the eucharist.

Life after Initiation

- The newly baptized continued living what they believed.

Egeria ◆ 11
Pilgrim and Diarist

While resting during her travels on horseback to the Holy Land (c. 381–384), Egeria kept a diary of her observations for her sisters back home in the religious community in Galicia, Spain. Mount Sinai, Constantinople and Bethlehem all welcomed her, as did Jerusalem. There she participated in the prayers of Holy Week, probably in the presence of the aging bishop Cyril (c. 315–c. 387), a man whose persistent love for the church kept him faithful through three different periods of exile.

Art Resource.

The Baptism of Constantine Pierre Puget (1620–94), Musée des Beaux-Arts, Marseille, France.

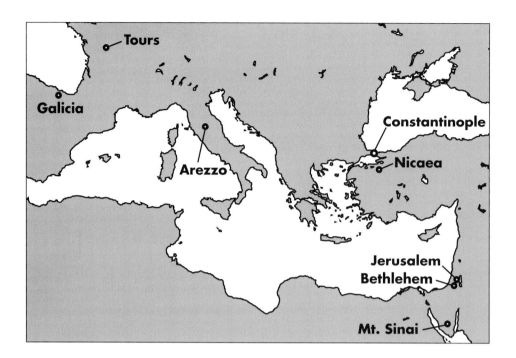

To Cyril is ascribed a collection of catechetical instructions offered to catechumens in preparation for baptism (c. 348–350). Another series of instruction for those who were newly baptized, the *Mystagogic Catecheses* (380–390), probably comes from his successor, John (+ 417).

During the reign of Constantine (306–338), Christianity had become the official religion of the Roman empire. As the numbers of converts increased, the catechumenate and baptism became more detailed. Jerusalem, the city of the death and resurrection of Christ, became a natural center for the baptismal ritual to develop. Constantine authorized the erection of the Church of the Holy Sepulcher over the sites of Golgotha and the tomb, reaching even to the ravine where legend has it that the relics of the true cross were found. Under that roof Egeria witnessed the baptisms over which Cyril very possibly presided.

A copy of Egeria's diary, lost for many years, was discovered in Arezzo, Italy, in 1884.

CATECHESIS

Neither Egeria nor Cyril say how people became catechumens, but their formation lasted for some time. Throughout that period Egeria notes that the bishop dismissed catechumens after morning prayer with a blessing every day (24). He prayed for and blessed them again at evening prayer. Some who applied for baptism were refused, presumably to wait another year. Catechumens were not permitted to attend the Easter week instructions, but received blessings as usual, notably on the Sunday after Easter (40) and on Pentecost (43). Not all catechumens were baptized each year; some remained in formation for the future.

The long period of formation culminated with the inscription of names. Egeria gives the first detailed description of this event. Often, in the history of baptismal preparation, the church intensified preparation immediately before baptism, but fourth-century Jerusalem finally shows evidence of a rite of passage to that stage.

Cyril refers to those who have been inscribed as *photizomenoi*, those who are going to be illumined. Egeria calls them *competentes*, those petitioning together for baptism. These are the earliest sources that distinguish by titles those near baptism from other catechumens.

On the evening before Lent began, according to Egeria (45), those who wished to be baptized gave their names to a presbyter. Lent, called "the forty days," lasted eight weeks because Saturday and Sunday were not days of fast (27). "When the presbyter has written down the names of all, after the next day of Lent, that is the day on which the eight weeks begin, a chair for the bishop is placed in the middle of the larger church, that is in the Martyrium. The presbyters sit in chairs on both sides and all the clerics stand. Those petitioning for baptism are brought in one by one. If they are men, they come with their godfathers. If they are women, they come with their godmothers. The bishop asks the neighbors of each man who has come up, 'Is he living a good life? Does he respect his parents? Is he a drunkard or a liar?' He investigates each one for all faults which are even more serious. And if the man is proven beyond reproach in all these matters which he placed before the witnesses present, the bishop writes down that man's name with his own hand. But if a man is accused by another, the bishop orders him to go outside, saying, 'He should mend his ways. When he has done so, then let him come back to the font.' He investigates the men in this way. Then he does the same with the women. If any are pilgrims they do not come easily to baptism unless they have witnesses who know them" (*Pilgrimage* 45). Although Cyril's own writings verified that Lent lasted forty days, referred to those whose names were inscribed (*Procatechesis* 1; 4) and made an allusion to godparents (*Catechesis* 15:18), he did not describe this event with similar detail.

Throughout the forty days those to be enlightened received special prayers and exhortations. Cyril urged them to come forward with pure motives, not because they had fallen in love with someone or sought some personal favor (*Procatechesis* 5). They were to accept this as a time for spiritual battle (*Procatechesis* 1). To help them, they performed good works (*Procatechesis* 4). Egeria (27) says catechumens fasted on Wednesdays and Fridays during Lent. They were expected to change their sinful behavior (*Procatechesis* 4) and spend time in prayer (*Procatechesis* 14). They underwent a series of exorcisms, with men and women in separate groups (*Procatechesis* 9; 14).

The catechumens' instruction was rooted in scripture. Cyril interpreted the assigned readings literally and figuratively. Those to be baptized learned about a proper spiritual demeanor, penance, the Ten Commandments, faith and the principal articles of the Creed—the Trinity and the resurrection of the body, for example (*Catecheses* 1–18). (The Council of Nicaea had formulated its Creed in 325.) It was a lot to learn, and some struggled to pay attention (*Procatechesis* 10).

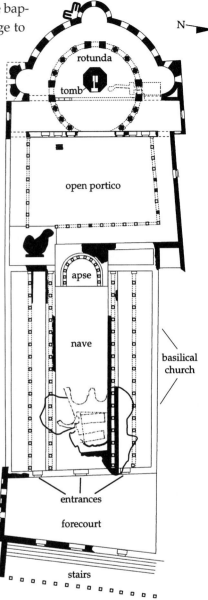

in Virgilio C. Corbo, *Il Santo Sepolcro di Gerusalemme: aspetti archeologici dalle origini al periodo crociato*, Jerusalem: Franciscan Printing Press, 1981. Courtesy Studium Biblicum Franciscanum.

Floor plan of the Church of the Holy Sepulcher, Jerusalem, fourth century.

PREPARATION FOR BAPTISM

Egeria says that during Lent (46) those to be baptized gathered at the Church of the Holy Sepulcher with their godparents and representatives of the faithful Monday through Friday, starting at dawn with an exorcism by the clergy. According to the *Mystagogic Catecheses*, the ministers breathed onto the catechumens during the exorcisms while invoking the name of God, to burn the devil like fire (2). The morning continued with catechetical instruction given by the bishop—for three hours. He spent five weeks on scripture, then those to be baptized received the Creed, and the bishop continued teaching on its themes for two more weeks (Egeria 46). Cyril (*Procatechesis* 12) and Egeria (47) concur that those receiving catechesis were supposed to keep quiet about what they learned. Only the baptized and those preparing for baptism were entitled to hear these secret instructions. Without the proper formation, others were unprepared to accept what they would hear.

"When seven weeks of Lent had passed and only Passover week remained, which is called the Great Week, the bishop comes in the morning at the larger church to the Martyrium. Back in the apse behind the altar a chair is placed for the bishop. Each man goes there with his father and each woman with her mother, and one by one they return the creed to the bishop" (*Pilgrimage* 46).

Because Egeria calls the sponsors "father" and "mother" at this point, she leaves open the possibility that children who recited the Creed to the bishop came with their parents. The bishop then delivered a homily. Throughout Holy Week catechumens received blessings daily (32–37).

BAPTISM

After all the detail she provides regarding the events leading to the Easter Vigil, Egeria, to the utter disappointment of later generations, succinctly summarizes the entire night for her sisters back home in one sentence: "They do the Easter Vigil here the way we do" (38). Information on the baptisms at Jerusalem comes from the mystagogic catecheses attributed to John. During Easter Week he looked back on the events and catechized the newly baptized; in doing so he left a record of ritual elements.

Baptism required several ritual stages. Just as baptismal preparation clearly coincided with Lent in Jerusalem, so baptism occurred on Easter. This connection gained special significance because of the location of the rites—in the city of Jesus' death, at the very place of his resurrection.

A baptistry was established outside the Church of the Holy Sepulcher. Before entering it, those who had petitioned

Sculpture: Kansas City (Missouri) Public Library. Photo: © 2000 Jack Denzer Photo Service.

Martin of Tours (316–97) as a catechumen, sharing his cloak with a beggar.

turned one by one to the west, raised their hands and renounced Satan, his empty promises, his works and worship. Then facing east, they raised their hands and professed their faith in God (*Mystagogic Catecheses* 1).

Once inside the baptistry, they removed their clothing and stood naked, like Christ on the cross, like Adam unashamed. They were anointed with olive oil "from the hairs of their head to the soles of their feet," grafting themselves onto the good olive tree of Jesus, in order to purge away sin and rout the power of the devil. Those to be baptized were led to the pool as Christ was led from the cross to the tomb. Then, confessing their belief in the Father, Son and Holy Spirit, those who had prepared for this day were immersed three times (*Mystagogic Catecheses* 2).

The newly baptized were anointed with chrism on their forehead, ears, nostrils and breast to be sanctified with the Holy Spirit. "Do not presume that this chrism is simple oil. After the prayer for the Holy Spirit the bread of the eucharist is no longer simple bread but the body of Christ. Just so with the prayer for the Holy Spirit this holy oil is no longer a pure and simple oil. It is the gift of Christ, made efficacious of his divinity by the presence of the Holy Spirit" (*Mystagogic Catecheses* 3). Having removed the old garments of sin and put on the new ones of Christian life, they were asked to keep their garments white all their days. This figurative reflection suggests that the newly baptized were given a white garment to wear (*Mystagogic Catecheses* 4).

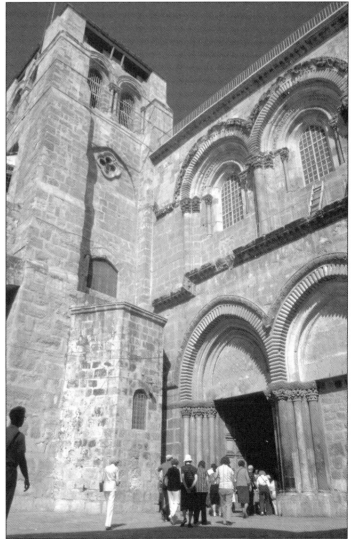

© 2000 Passionist Research Center.

Egeria describes only one part of the baptismal rite because it differed from her experience at home. After the newly baptized came up from the font and dressed, they were brought to the bishop, who was seated by the tomb of Christ, where he prayed for them. Then they entered the larger church with the bishop, to join the community keeping vigil (38).

At the altar for the eucharist all exchanged a kiss of reconciliation. The bishop recited the eucharistic prayer. All prayed the Lord's Prayer and shared in communion under both forms. While their lips were still wet with the blood of Christ, the people moistened their fingers with it and touched their forehead, eyes and other organs of sense (*Mystagogic Catecheses* 5).

LIFE AFTER INITIATION

Egeria reports that during Easter Week the newly baptized joined the community and the bishop for daily prayers (39). Every day that

South entrance of the Church of the Holy Sepulcher, possible location of its fourth-century baptismal font.

week the bishop, inside the church, leaning against the rail above the tomb of Christ, explained to the newly baptized the meaning of their baptism (47). Only the baptized were welcomed to these catecheses. They were so moved by his instruction that people outside the building heard their shouts of approval. The bishop spoke in Greek, but translators interpreted his talks for those who spoke Syriac or Latin.

◆◆◆

Egeria and Cyril together give a picture of initiation in the Jerusalem church. Egeria reports two ritual actions missing in Cyril: the enrollment of names and the recitation of the Creed; information on the baptismal rites comes mainly from the mystagogic catecheses of the bishop. None of these sources explicitly mentions blessings for the oil of catechumens, chrism, or water, nor the postbaptismal imposition of hands, although these ceremonies could have happened unrecorded.

Catechesis

• Catechumens were blessed and dismissed daily from public worship.

• Formation may have lasted over a year.

Preparation for Baptism

• Those seeking baptism gave their names to a presbyter on the Saturday before Lent began.

• On the First Sunday of Lent the bishop received testimony about the character of those requesting baptism. Godparents presented them. The bishop personally wrote down the names of those he accepted for baptism.

• Those chosen for baptism were called "those to be enlightened" *(photizomenoi)* or "those petitioning together for baptism" *(competentes).*

• They fasted and amended their behavior.

• Clergy exorcised them every morning.

• They received daily instruction for five weeks on the scriptures and for two weeks on the Creed.

• On the Sunday before Easter those to be baptized recited the Creed to the bishop.

• They received blessings each day during Holy Week.

Baptism

- Those to be baptized renounced Satan while facing west and professed faith in God while facing east.

- They removed their clothing and received an anointing.

- "Those petitioning together" were baptized in the name of the Trinity, by immersion, in a font outside the church.

- They were anointed with chrism and clothed.

- They entered the church and went to the bishop, who prayed for them.

- They joined the community for the eucharist: the kiss, the Lord's Prayer and communion.

Life after Initiation

- Throughout Easter Week the newly baptized prayed with the community and received special instructions from the bishop about the meaning of their baptism.

- They kept these teachings from the uninitiated.

12 ◆ Ambrose
Catechumen and Bishop

Ambrose was still a catechumen when the people of Milan selected him to be their bishop. Born in Trier in 339, he moved to Rome after his father died. There he received the education he needed to follow his father's footsteps into politics. Ambrose became a governor in northern Italy around the age of 30. Three years later, the bishop of Milan died. The people were so inspired with Ambrose's civic leadership that they chose him to become their spiritual shepherd. He was ordained shortly after his baptism, and by the time of his death in 397 he had become one of the greatest pastors and catechists of the Western church.

Fabbrica Duomo Milano.

Ruins of the baptistry of Saint Ambrose, Milan, fourth century.

Three of Ambrose's works center on baptism. His *Explanation of the Creed* (c. 385) contains the teachings he offered before baptism. *Sacraments* (c. 380) is a dictation of his postbaptismal sermons, which he appears to have edited in *Mysteries* (c. 390). Allusions to baptismal formation also occur in several others of his works.

CATECHESIS

Ambrose did not record how a person first entered the cate-chumenate. In *Mysteries* (20) he says that the catechumen believed in the cross of the Lord Jesus and was signed by it. A signing could have accompanied one's entrance into the catechumenate or a later occasion in formation.

PREPARATION FOR BAPTISM

Baptismal formation began with an inscription of names. Ambrose expected catechumens to give their names to him for baptism during the Epiphany season, and he complained to God when they did not (*Exposition on the Gospel according to Luke* 4:76). At the inscription the minister took mud and smeared it on the eyes of those giving their names (cf. John 9:7), a sign of the blindness caused by their sin (*Sacraments* 3:12). From this point Ambrose called those preparing for baptism "those petitioning" (see, for example, *Letter* 76:4) and "the elect" (as in *Elijah and Fasting* 10:34). His contemporary Pope Siricius also used the term "elect" in his first letter to Himerius of Tarragon in 385, where he stated that they received the title at least forty days before baptism, during a period marked by fasting, prayer and exorcism.

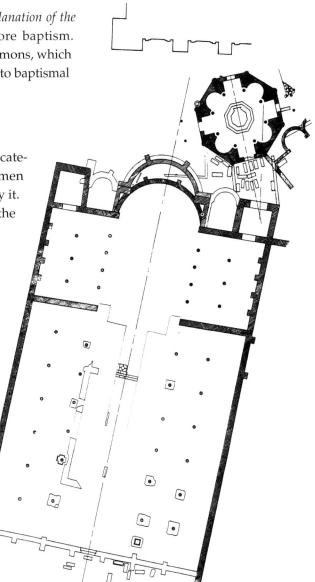

Courtesy Edizioni ET, Milano.

Floor plan of the Basilica of Saint Thecla, Milan, with baptistry used by Saint Ambrose.

Throughout this time, Ambrose urged catechumens to eat and drink sparingly, to be chaste in body and to avoid the games (*Elijah and Fasting* 21:79). They were like athletes in formation, Ambrose said, and he urged them to medi-tate, to exercise and to be anointed daily (*Elijah and Fasting* 21:79). They received a daily sermon on morals, based on the scriptures of the patriarchs and proverbs (*Mysteries* 1).

Baptismal formation continued with scrutinies. The holiness of the candi-dates was examined with exorcisms of their body and spirit. "So far the mysteries of the scrutinies have been celebrated. These sought out whether impurities clung to anyone's body. Through the exorcism not only of the body but also of the soul, sanctification was searched for and grasped. Now is the time and day that we pre-sent the creed" (*Explanation of the Creed* 1).

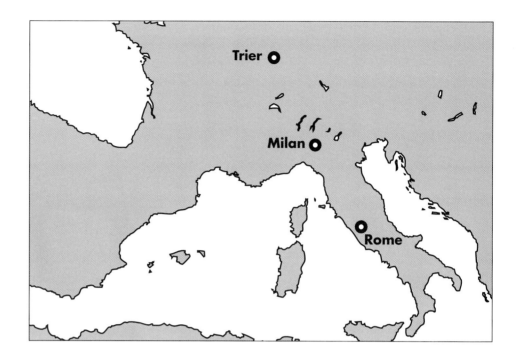

A series of three scrutinies had developed in Rome by this time, according to the *Canons for the Gauls* (c. 400), which stated that the anointings repeated on those occasions manifested the power and grace of God (11).

These were followed on a Sunday just before Easter by the presentation of the Creed (*Letter* 76:4), delivered to the elect after the catechumens had been dismissed. Its presentation occasioned the delivery of the *Explanation* by Ambrose (1). The faithful memorized the Creed and never wrote it down, to keep it close to their hearts (9).

The baptismal rite began on the Vigil of Easter outside the baptistry with the "mystery of the opening," or the *ephphetha*. In this rite, already evidenced in the *Apostolic Tradition*, the bishop touched the eyes and nose of the one to be baptized. Ambrose drew a comparison to Mark 7:34, where Jesus healed a blind man with a speech impediment. He says the bishop touched the nose, not the lips, because the newly baptized would inhale the sweet odor of eternal devotion (cf. 2 Corinthians 2:15), and because it was not proper for a man to touch a woman's lips (*Sacraments* 1:2–3; *Mysteries* 3–4).

A procession moved to the font. There the presbyter anointed the elect all over, as athletes preparing for a contest (*Sacraments* 1:4; *Mysteries* 6). They renounced Satan in response to questions (*Sacraments* 1:6; *Mysteries* 7) and then turned east toward Christ. The presbyter exorcised the water (*Sacraments* 1:18). Ambrose then gives an extended explanation of the scriptural images of baptism (*Sacraments* 1:9–22; *Mysteries* 8–19). The water blessing became an opportunity for baptismal catechesis.

For baptism, the elect heard three questions: "Do you believe in God the Father almighty? Do you believe in our Lord Jesus Christ and in his cross? Do you believe in the Holy Spirit." Each time they answered "I believe," and each time they were immersed in water (*Sacraments 2:20; Mysteries* 28). Archeologists have uncovered the remains of the eight-sided font Ambrose used.

Coming up from the font, the newly baptized went to the bishop, who anointed them with chrism "in the reign of God and in the spiritual grace of priests" (*Sacraments* 2:24; *Mysteries* 29–30). After the gospel of Jesus washing the feet of his disciples (John 13:1–15) was proclaimed, the bishop washed the feet of the newly baptized (*Sacraments* 3:4; *Mysteries* 33).

The bishop then prayed that the newly baptized would receive the sevenfold gift of the Holy Spirit, a spiritual sign (*Sacraments* 3:8). "Recall that you received a spiritual sign, 'the spirit of wisdom and understanding, the spirit of counsel and strength, the spirit of knowledge and piety, the spirit of holy fear' (Isaiah 11:2–3), and preserve what you have received. God the Father has signed you, Christ the Lord has confirmed you and given the pledge of the spirit in your hearts, as you have learned in the apostolic reading (2 Corinthians 1:21–22)" (*Mysteries* 42). This is the earliest reference to a most influential prayer.

> **God the almighty Father, who has given you rebirth by water and the Spirit and forgiven your sins, himself anoints you for eternal life.**
>
> *Sacraments 2:24*

The baptized received white garments as a sign of their rebirth (*Sacraments* 5:14; *Mysteries* 34; *Exposition on the Gospel according to Luke* 5:25). Approaching the altar, then, they celebrated the eucharist with the bishop. They acclaimed "Amen" and received communion (*Sacraments* 4:25; *Mysteries* 54). Ambrose concludes with an explanation of the Lord's Prayer (*Sacraments* 5:18–30).

Life after Initiation

In the days after Easter, the bishop delivered a series of instructions to the newly baptized, from which comes most of this information about their baptism. These mystagogic catecheses presume that the catechumens were not told about the mysteries they celebrated until after they were baptized. Catechumens were not expected to know the meaning of baptism, the eucharist and the other rites before they were initiated. In fact, they were forbidden to know about them. The explanations came later.

◆◆◆

Catechesis

- Catechesis incorporated a signation, possibly at the start.

Preparation for Baptism

- Those seeking baptism submitted their names during the Epiphany season, when a minister smeared mud on their eyes. Afterwards they were called "those petitioning" or "the elect."

- Preparation included prayer, exorcisms and scrutinies, ascetic practices and instruction on the moral life.

- Three scrutinies had developed in Rome.

- On a Sunday shortly before Easter the community presented the Creed orally to those chosen for baptism.

Baptism

- Outside the baptistry the bishop conducted the ephphetha rite, touching those to be baptized on the eyes and nose.

- A presbyter anointed them all over.

- They renounced Satan, then faced east to profess faith in Christ.

- The water was exorcised.

- The elect were baptized in a triple immersion, confessing faith in God, Jesus and the Holy Spirit.

- The bishop anointed them with chrism.

- The bishop washed their feet.

- The bishop invoked the sevenfold gift of the Holy Spirit.

- The newly baptized were dressed in white garments.

- They celebrated eucharist with the bishop.

Life after Initiation

- After Easter the bishop explained to the newly baptized what they had celebrated, including a catechesis on the Lord's Prayer.

Augustine ◆ 13
Convert and Catalyst

Augustine, the future bishop, and Adeodatus, the fifteen-year-old son he had fathered out of wedlock, were baptized together in Milan by Ambrose in 387. In 391, Augustine was ordained a priest in Hippo, in modern-day Algeria, and became bishop of the city a few years later. Born in 354 of a saintly mother, Monica, and a father who received baptism shortly before his death, Augustine was made a catechumen as an infant but delayed his baptism in favor of living a more self-centered life. He kept a mistress, affiliated himself with the Manichee sect for nine years and taught rhetoric before he heard Ambrose in Milan and sought baptism. As bishop, Augustine became one of the most prolific, articulate and influential writers in the history of the church and of philosophy.

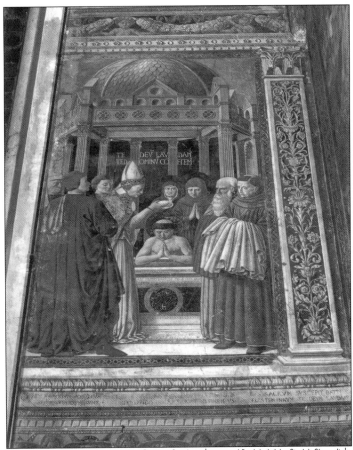

Ambrose Baptizing Augustine by Benozzo Gozzoli, 1464, San Gimignano, Italy.

References to the catechumenate and to baptism abound in his writings. A survey of them reveals a picture of an intense period of formation punctuated by a series of rich liturgical celebrations.

FIRST INTEREST

According to Augustine, everyone desiring to become a Christian approached the church out of some fear of God. But some came because of lesser motives: to coax an advantage from someone or avoid a disadvantage from another. Nonetheless, a skilled catechist could purify the motives of all who presented themselves. Augustine suggested that the catechist should learn the candidates' motives, either from people who knew them or by questioning the candidates in a personal interview (*Catechizing Beginners* 5:9).

I was already signed with the sign of his cross and preserved with his salt since coming from the womb of my mother. *Confessions* 1:11

During this interview, a preliminary catechesis followed the investigation of motives. If the candidate appeared sincere, the catechist expounded a lengthy summary of Christian teaching on the spot, including the beliefs and moral precepts of the church (16:24—25:49). A shorter presentation could also be made (26:51—27:55). Some candidates already had formed themselves in the basics of Christianity before expressing their intention to become a Christian; if so, the catechist could abbreviate the instruction, while strengthening their motives (8:12).

CATECHESIS

If the candidates believed these matters and desired to observe them, they were solemnly signed (26:50). This ritual marked their entrance into catechumenal formation. Catechumens were also given salt, either as a symbol of preservation or as a foretaste of the eucharist.

Christian infants could be claimed for Christ, even though their baptism would come later. Augustine himself was signed with the cross and given salt as an infant, but did not seek baptism until he was 33 (*Confessions* 1:11).

During their formation, catechumens strove to change any sinful behavior that kept them from Christ. Augustine did not concur with those who argued that baptism should be given to all, saints and sinners alike, and that sinners should be exhorted to change their lives after baptism. Behavioral change is what pre-baptismal formation accomplished (*Faith and Works* 1:1; 13:19).

To fulfill their aspirations, catechumens could attend the word service with the faithful, but did not partake of the eucharist. Augustine hoped their curiosity would provoke them to commit themselves to Christ (*Sermon* 132:1).

PREPARATION FOR BAPTISM

Several weeks before Easter, the catechumens who sought baptism submitted their names. Augustine prodded them (see, for example, *Sermon* 132:1 and *Commentary on the Psalms* 80:8), but he does not describe exactly how or when this inscription took place.

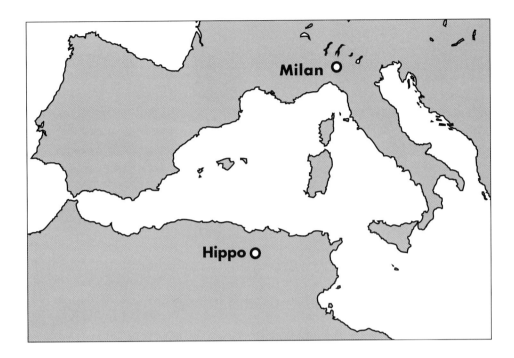

Catechumens prepared for baptism during the forty days of Lent by fasting, vigils, exorcisms and abstinence from food, drink and sexual intercourse (*Sermon* 229A:2; *Faith and Works* 6:8). During the scrutiny rites, the ministers exorcised the catechumens, even the children, with exsufflations, that is, by blowing upon them. Catechumens renounced Satan and stood on sackcloth or goatskin as a sign of their repentance and humiliation (*Sermons* 215:1; 216:6, 10–11; 227). Augustine does not state precisely when during Lent these rites occurred.

Probably two weeks before Easter, Augustine solemnly presented the Creed to those preparing for baptism. He preached about its meaning and urged his hearers never to write down the Creed. Those to be baptized were to report the following week to "return" the Creed to Augustine by reciting it individually. In those eight days, with assistance from the community, they memorized it, phrase by phrase (*Sermons* 212–215). In Rome, catechumens customarily returned the Creed while standing on a raised platform in front of all the people, though the nervous and fearful could do so in private (*Confessions* 8:2). If they failed to deliver it properly, Augustine gave them another chance the following Saturday, the morning of the baptisms (*Sermon* 58:1).

On the day they returned the Creed (*Sermon* 213:9), catechumens received the Lord's Prayer (*Sermons* 56–59). The prayer was proclaimed in the reading from Matthew 6:9–13, and in this manner the Lord's Prayer was presented to the catechumens (*Sermon* 59:1). They then repeated it before the community every day for a week (*Sermons* 58:1; 59:1). "You have not received first the Lord's Prayer and then the Creed, but first the Creed, where you may know what you believe, and then the Prayer, where you know whom you entreat" (*Sermon* 56:1).

On the Saturday morning before the Easter Vigil, those to be baptized pronounced their faith in the Creed (*Sermon* 58:13). The community joined them in their fast (*Sermon* 210:2).

© 1989, Loyola University Chicago Archives: R. V. Schoder, SJ, photographer.

Ruins of Basilica of Saint Augustine, fourth century, Hippo Regius, apse and crypt.

BAPTISM

Baptisms ordinarily took place at the Easter Vigil, and by exception at any other time (*Sermon* 210:1). Augustine urged the entire community to keep vigil with those about to be baptized, listening to the scriptures and speaking aloud in prayer (*Sermon* 219).

At the time of baptism, men and women separated at the font (*The City of God* 22:8). The water was blessed (*Baptism* 6:25, 47), and each was asked if he or she believed in the Trinity (*Letters of Petilian* 3:8, 9) and in the church (*Baptism* 5:20, 28). Those who held children represented the whole community by whose faith the children received the grace of baptism, and they answered the minister's questions on behalf of the children (*Letter* 98:7). "Children are offered to receive spiritual grace not so much by those in whose hands they are carried (though also by them if they themselves are good believers) but by the whole gathering of saints and faithful" (*Letter* 98:5). Those to be baptized descended into the water (*Sermon* 258:2) and were dipped into it as into a cleansing bath (*Sermon* 213:9). In those waters they were buried with Christ (*Sermon* 229A:1). The minister baptized in the name of the Trinity (*Baptism* 3:15, 20; *Letter* 23:4; *Letters of Petilian* 2:87, 178).

That the baptized were anointed can be surmised from Augustine's references to anointing in a baptismal context (*Sermon* 227; *Letters of Petilian* 2:104, 237). "Then came baptism with water. You (the wheat) were 'moistened', so to speak, so that you might come into the form of bread. But there is no bread yet without fire. So what does fire connote? Chrism. For the oil of our fire, of the Holy Spirit, is a sacrament. . . . So the Holy Spirit comes next, fire after water, and you become the bread which is the body of Christ" (*Sermon* 227). He also says the sevenfold gift of the Holy Spirit was called down upon the newly baptized (*Sermons* 229M:2; 249:3) during an imposition of hands (*Tract on the Letter of John* 6:10).

Look, it is passover. Give your name for baptism.

If the feast does not move you, let curiosity itself

lead you. *Sermon* 132:1

After baptism, the "infants," as Augustine called the newly baptized, were clothed in white (*Sermons* 223:1; 260C:7). They wore these garments together with a head covering all Easter week. They also sported some kind of footwear that week, so their bare feet would never touch the ground (*Letter* 55:35).

The vigil reached its climax with participation in the eucharist. The "infants" recited the Lord's Prayer with the assembly and exchanged the kiss of peace

(*Sermons* 227; 229:3). At communion they answered Amen to what they believed (*Sermon* 272) and received under both forms (*Sermon* 262:3). Infant children received as well as adults (*Letter* 217:5,16).

LIFE AFTER INITIATION

The education of the newly baptized continued throughout the week (*Sermons* 230–239), beginning on Easter morning (see, for example, *Sermon* 228). During this time the neophytes, or "new sprouts," learned about baptism and the eucharist and were exhorted to lead a faithful Christian life.

Although Ambrose included the washing of feet in the baptismal rite, Augustine knew communities that celebrated it on the Tuesday or Sunday after Easter, to distinguish it from baptism, and to sanctify the symbolic third and eighth days (*Letter* 55:33).

◆◆◆

A survey of Augustine's work shows an intentional catechumenate and a rich celebration of baptism.

First Interest

- People sought baptism out of a fear of God or for lesser motives of personal advantage.

- The catechist conducted an initial conversation and instruction to test motives.

Catechesis

- Catechesis began with a solemn ritual involving a signation and salt.

- Some became catechumens as infants and remained in that stage for many years.

- Catechumens attended the word service with the faithful but not the eucharist.

- Catechumens purified their behaviors.

Preparation for Baptism

- Those who desired baptism submitted their names to the bishop some weeks before Easter.

- During Lent they were exorcised and practiced abstinence in food, drink, sex and sleep.

- Scrutiny rites reinforced the exorcisms.

- Two weeks before Easter the bishop presented the Creed to the catechumens and explained its meaning. They were asked not to write it down, but to memorize it and recite it back to him the following week.

- On the day they returned the Creed, catechumens received the Lord's Prayer.

Baptism

- On Saturday morning the community joined the catechumens in fast and they professed their faith in the Creed.

- All gathered with the catechumens for the Easter Vigil.

- Women and men separated.

- Water was blessed.

- Those to be baptized answered questions about their faith in the Trinity and in the church.

- Members of the community presented the children and answered for them.

- Baptism was by immersion in the name of the Trinity.

- The newly baptized were anointed with oil.

- The bishop imposed hands on them and prayed for the sevenfold gifts of the Holy Spirit.

- They put on special garments.

- They participated in the eucharist.

Life after Initiation

- The bishop continued catechizing the newly baptized throughout the week of Easter.

- They wore their baptismal garments that week.

- In some communities the newly baptized had their feet washed on the third or eighth day of baptism.

John Chrysostom ◆ 14
Preacher and Patriarch

A preacher so talented they called him "Golden Mouth," John ended his days as a deposed patriarch. Born in Antioch (c. 344), the capital of Syria, he studied philosophy and literature. After his baptism he sought more religious formation and began four years of scripture study while living in strict asceticism. John was ordained a priest in 386 and earned his reputation as "Chrysostom" because of his homilies. Among those, several pertain to baptism, dating from 388 and 390. Chosen to be patriarch of Constantinople in 397, John recommended reforms for the clergy, the laity and the court. Opposed by Theophilus of Alexandria, the empress Theodosia and an array of bishops, John was exiled twice and removed from his office. He died without honors in 407, but he is remembered among the saints as one of the greatest doctors of the Eastern church.

Saint John Chrysostom, mosaic icon from Constantinople, c. 1325 or later.

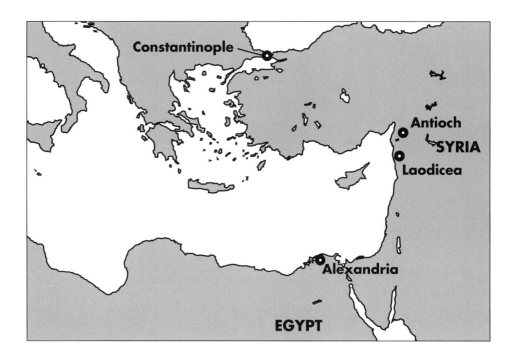

CATECHESIS

John Chrysostom placed catechumens and the faithful in completely different categories. "They do not have the same head, nor the same father, nor the same city, nor food, nor clothing, nor table. Everything is separate" (*Homily 25 on John* 3). His works never tell how people first became catechumens, but when the faithful gathered, the deacon invited all to pray for them as they were dismissed from their assembly (*Homily 30 on 2 Corinthians* 5–8).

PREPARATION FOR BAPTISM

Intense preparation for baptism took place during the season of Lent. Near its beginning, those who wished to be baptized submitted their names. Although this inscription probably occurred over a period of some days, it should have been completed before Chrysostom gave his first catechetical address thirty days before Easter (*Three Baptismal Catecheses* 1:2). He says nothing more about the inscription for the candidates he would now call "those being enlightened."

I said before and I say now and I will not cease to say that if any have not corrected their sinful behaviors nor prepared themselves for effortless rectitude, they will not be baptized. *Catechesis* 2:2

Throughout their time of preparation, those being enlightened worked to change their behavior with the help of Chrysostom's instructions. He urged them to avoid swearing (*Eight Baptismal Catecheses* 1:2), to adorn the face with modesty rather than jewelry (*Two Baptismal Catecheses* 2:4), to abstain from public entertainment (*Two Baptismal Catecheses* 2:5), fortune-telling (*Three Baptismal Catecheses* 1:39) and the like. They should avoid worldly concerns, be extremely chaste, and zealous to meditate only on the mysteries for which they were preparing (*Three Baptismal Catecheses* 1:6). All the faithful fasted during Lent, as did even the catechumens who would not be baptized that year (*Responses to the Jews* 3). Above all,

Chrysostom asked those being enlightened to abstain from sin (*Eight Baptismal Catecheses* 5:2). Failure to do so would jeopardize their baptism (*Two Baptismal Catecheses* 2:2).

John encouraged this behavior by means of pre-baptismal instructions. Besides these moral exhortations, he also interpreted some of the baptismal rites; unlike many of his predecessors, John did not wait until after baptism to explain them.

> **Godparents know well that good repute will return to them if by their personal encouragement they lead those who have been entrusted to them in the way of virtue. If on the other hand they are negligent, they themselves will undergo a serious condemnation.** *Catechesis* 2:16

Godparents had the responsibility of bearing testimony on behalf of those being enlightened. Chrysostom solemnly urged them to take this charge seriously. Godparents were like those who testify to creditors about the borrower's reputation; they had to guarantee the good behavior of their charges, even after baptism (*Eight Baptismal Catecheses* 2:15–16).

Those approaching baptism were exorcised every day after the instruction to purify their spirit, to impress the soul with devotion, and to force the devil to depart from them in haste (*Eight Baptismal Catecheses* 2:12). As Easter approached they removed their shoes and their outer clothes and, dressed only in loincloths, formed a procession toward the shouts of the exorcists (*Three Baptismal Catecheses* 1:7).

Chrysostom does not say whether or not those preparing for baptism received or returned the Creed.

At three o'clock on Good Friday afternoon, at the hour when the Good Thief won paradise by his confession of faith, those to be baptized made their solemn contract. They knelt, lifted their hands and prayed (*Three Baptismal Catecheses* 3:4). They renounced Satan and professed their allegiance to Christ (3:6). This pronouncement was followed by an anointing with chrism on the forehead in the name of the Trinity with the sign of the cross (*Eight Baptismal Catecheses* 2:22–23).

BAPTISM

For the baptismal vigil, the priest removed all the clothing from those to be baptized, and their entire bodies were anointed to strengthen them and shield them from the devil (2:24). Chrysostom makes no mention of a water blessing. He brought those to be baptized into flowing waters; they entered naked, to recall the innocence of Adam and Eve (*Three Baptismal Catecheses* 3:8). He placed his hand on each one's head (*Eight Baptismal Catecheses* 2:25), announced their name, "N. is baptized in the name of the Father and of the Son and of the Holy Spirit," and plunged them three times into the water. By using the passive voice, Chrysostom stressed that it was not the minister who baptized, but the Trinity (2:26).

Coming up from the pool, the newly baptized received the embrace, greeting and kiss of the community, who congratulated them and shared their happiness. Chrysostom reports no anointing following baptism. Although the early Syrian tradition placed the anointing before baptism, the Council of Laodicea in Syria (c. 381) requested a postbaptismal anointing, probably to resemble more closely the pattern emerging in the rest of the church. "Those who are enlightened should be anointed with heavenly chrism after baptism and become participants in the reign of Christ" (*Council of Laodicea* 48). Although Chrysostom's commentaries date from after that time, he still had not incorporated the postbaptismal anointing.

All then participated in the eucharist. "They are brought to the illustrious table, laden with a thousand gifts. They taste the body and blood of the Lord and become the dwelling of the Spirit. They have put on Christ, and wherever they go they appear like earth angels, as radiant as sunshine" (*Eight Baptismal Catecheses* 2:27).

LIFE AFTER INITIATION

Throughout the week after Easter the newly baptized received instructions on the Christian life and celebrated the eucharist (*Eight Baptismal Catecheses* 6:24).

◆◆◆

In Antioch, John Chrysostom gave a rich description of the initiation rites.

Catechesis

• Deacons dismissed catechumens from the liturgy with a blessing.

Preparation for Baptism

• Those who desired baptism submitted their names around the beginning of Lent and became known as "those being enlightened."

• For thirty days before baptism they received instructions on how to live and about the rites they would celebrate.

• The daily instructions were followed by an exorcism.

• Those preparing for baptism accepted penitential disciplines during Lent.

• Godparents assisted the preparation and guaranteed the behavior of those to be baptized.

Baptism

• On Good Friday those to be baptized gathered, renounced Satan, professed their allegiance to Christ, and were anointed with chrism by a cross on the forehead in the name of the Trinity.

• During the baptismal vigil their clothing was removed, they were anointed all over their bodies and immersed three times in the name of the Trinity with a formula spoken in the passive voice, "N. is baptized. . . ."

• Coming up from the water, they were congratulated by the community, who gave them the kiss of peace and shared eucharist with them. No postbaptismal anointing is mentioned.

Life after Initiation

• During Easter week the newly baptized received additional instructions and participated in the eucharist every day.

Theodore of
Mopsuestia
Homilist and Catechist

The Second Council of Constantinople condemned Theodore of Mopsuestia in 553, more than a hundred years after his death, because the Nestorians were building their heresy upon some of his teachings about Christ. During his life, though, Theodore was regarded as a great bishop and teacher. Born in Antioch around the year 350, he was ordained a priest in 383; in 392 he became bishop of Mopsuestia in Cilicia, about a hundred miles from Antioch, near the city of Tarsus, at the modern border of Syria and Turkey. Mopsuestia's fame in the patristic literature rests primarily upon this bishop. By the time of his death in 428 he had left behind an impressive body of homilies.

Courtesy Verlag der Österreichische Akademie der Wissenchaften.

Remains of cruciform baptismal font, Haciömerli, Cilicia, early sixth century. This is located near Misis, the present-day site of the ancient city of Mopsuestia.

Those homilies that pertain to baptism had been lost until 1931, when Alphonse Mingana (1878–1937) published them. Mingana, son of a Chaldean priest in northern Iraq, joined the French Dominicans in Mosul. A student of languages, he eventually settled at Woodbrooke, England, a center for Quaker studies, where he continued his work. On research expeditions to Iraq and Egypt in the 1920s he gathered an extensive collection of Syrian and Arabic manuscripts, including the lost baptismal homilies of Theodore of Mopsuestia. Scholars differ in their opinion about the dating of the homilies; some say they come from Theodore's career as a priest in Antioch before 392; others say he delivered these talks in Mopsuestia in 420.

The sixteen homilies include the ten that explain the Creed, and six on what he calls the sacraments: one on the Lord's Prayer, three on baptism, and one on the eucharist. Only the last two were clearly delivered after baptism; the others formed part of prebaptismal instruction.

These sixteen homilies were delivered over the space of several weeks. Some of the homilies indicate the time intervals: The second followed the day after the first (2:1); three days separated the sixth from the seventh (7:1); the eleventh came the day after the tenth (11:1). They all could easily have filled the weeks between inscription and baptism.

Theodore gives no information about catechumenal formation prior to the immediate preparation for baptism.

PREPARATION FOR BAPTISM

Those who desired baptism gave their names to the one in charge of this procedure, who would also receive testimony from their godparents about their behavior. Godparents were baptized members of the community who acted as witnesses and guides for those who sought participation in the "heavenly city" of which they were members. If the testimony was favorable, the one in charge wrote down the names both of the catechumens and of the godparents (12:14–16).

Those seeking baptism presented themselves to the exorcists. Theodore regarded this step as "absolutely essential." He interprets the exorcism as a trial in court. Satan has laid claim to the catechumens, which accounts for their former evil behavior; the exorcists argue that Christ has conquered death. God ultimately renders judgment against Satan in favor of the exorcists (12:18–22). Throughout the entire trial, those seeking baptism, the "plaintiffs" in the case, observed silence. They removed their outer clothes and knelt upright on goatskin, bowed their heads and extended their hands like beggars to obtain mercy from the judge (12:23–25).

At some point the Creed was "placed upon the lips" of those to be baptized. They were admonished to concern their spirits with the words of the Creed to fix it in their minds. Without it they could not receive the divine gift nor hold it firmly (12:25). The first ten prebaptismal homilies all explain its verses. They suggest that the Creed was presented shortly after inscription, but Theodore does not describe how this was done.

Theodore does recount, however, the catechumens' recitation of the Creed. After a series of exorcisms, this ritual demonstrated one's shift in allegiance from Satan to God. It took place in the presence of the bishop (12:27). If people desire a

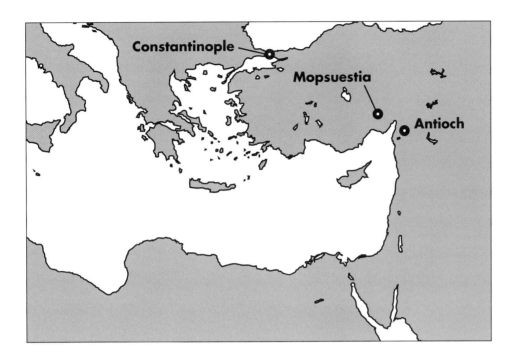

position in a large house, Theodore argues, they present themselves not to the owner, but to the administrator. So when people present themselves to the house of God, they go to the administrator, the bishop.

Theodore does not report a presentation of the Lord's Prayer. However, the eleventh homily is devoted to an explanation of the text.

As the time for the sacraments approached, those to be baptized renounced Satan. They assumed a posture similar to the one for exorcism. Having removed their outer garments and shoes, they knelt upright on a haircloth. This time, though, they lifted their hands to God in an attitude of prayer and raised their faces toward heaven. Addressing God, they renounced Satan, his angels, works and service, and they pledged their faith in the Trinity.

Theodore explained the significance of the renunciation. In renouncing Satan, people affirm that they once took his side, but now they have turned toward God. The angels of Satan are those who received evil from him and shared it with others: poets of idolatry, pagan philosophers and leaders of heresies. Theodore names names: Mani, Marcion, Valentin, Paul of Samosate, Arius, Eunomius and Apollinarus. The services of Satan included pagan sacrifices, adoration of idols, and whatever led to the corruption of souls, such as astrology and a magical interpretation of nature. Theodore also forbade entertainments like the theater, games of ridicule, the circus, games of combat, athletics, songs, hydraulic organs and dance, which the devil

Those who wish to come to the gift of holy baptism should present themselves to the church of God. They will be received by the one appointed for it, according to the established custom that those who come to baptism should be inscribed. The one who receives the names will be told about their behaviors. This responsibility is filed by those who are baptized, by those called "certifiers."

Now the one who is appointed for this writes in the book of the church and adds to your name in the book that also of the witness or the "guide" of this city or of that discipline. *Homily* 12

At its purchase a sheep receives the mark by which one knows to which master it belongs. It grazes in the same pasture and lives in the same fold as those on whom the same mark has been placed, indicating that they belong to the same master. Also when a soldier has been chosen worthy for service to the king because of his size and build, he first receives a mark on his hand to show which king he forever serves. Thus, you who have been chosen now for the reign of heaven can also be identified on examination as a soldier of the heavenly king.

Homily 13:17

"sows in the world under the appearance of amusement in order to arouse the human soul to its own deprivation." All these the catechumens renounced (13:5–13).

Belief in God, on the other hand, also constituted belief in the invisible and ineffable spiritual benefits that would come to the faithful. Those who professed faith said, "I believe and I am baptized in the name of the Father and of the Son and of the Holy Spirit." The faith in the Trinity was the faith of their baptism. That faith perceived this world as a symbol of the world to come, and baptism admitted one to citizenship in that world and its spiritual blessings (13:14–15).

After those to be baptized confessed their faith, the bishop, wearing brilliant vestments, signed their foreheads with oil in the name of the Trinity. The brilliance of the bishop's vestments indicated the glory of the world to come (13:17). This anointing with the cross signed them as a sheep of Christ, as a soldier of the heavenly king.

After the anointing, the godparents, standing behind, unfolded a linen cloth over their heads; this signified the free state they possessed, having been liberated from the grasp of Satan. Free citizens commonly wore one at home and in the market (13:19).

The godparents then lifted them and helped them stand up. Someone told the catechumens, as the angel who appeared to Cornelius had said to him (Acts 10:3), that their prayers had been heard.

Theodore does not say exactly when this renunciation, confession and anointing took place. It immediately preceded baptism, possibly on a distinct occasion. Chrysostom had a ceremony like this on Good Friday, but Theodore tells nothing about the date.

BAPTISM

The liturgy of baptism followed, a symbol of new birth. Those to be baptized stripped completely, in imitation of Adam, who knew no shame, and in order to be born again to immortality. They were anointed all over with oil, a sign of the garment of immortality they would receive in baptism. The bishop proclaimed that they were anointed in the name of the Trinity (14:8). The bishop blessed the water, making it a womb for rebirth, and those to be baptized entered it (14:9). The bishop, wearing his brilliant vestment, stood and laid his hand on them. He baptized in the name of the Trinity (14:14).

"N. is baptized in the name of the Father and of the Son and of the Holy Spirit." *Homily* 14:14

As he pronounced the names of the Trinity, he pushed the catechumens down into the water three times; catechumens submitted by bowing their heads, showing their consent to the bishop's words (14:18–20).

Coming up from the font, the newly baptized donned dazzling garments of pure white, a sign of the new life they shared (14:26).

The bishop then sealed them on the forehead in the name of the Trinity. He may have used oil, though Theodore does not say so explicitly as he does with other anointings. Instead, he compares the ritual to the anointing of Jesus with the Holy Spirit at his baptism, which, of course, involved no oil (14:27).

Afterward the newly baptized joined the community for the eucharist. They exchanged the kiss of peace (15:39–41), heard the eucharistic prayer (16:2–14) and received the body and blood of Christ. Extending their hands as the bishop said, "The body of Christ," they answered "Amen" and did the same when they were offered the cup. After communion all gave thanks to God in common (16:28–29).

> *After we recite the Creed before the bishop, it is by him that we make an accord and agreements with God. It is to God that we promise to be submitted in these professions of faith, to serve him and to persevere forever and to protect his love continually without alteration. . . . Thus we obtain the privilege of entering the house, of seeing, knowing, and living in this place. We have great protection in this city where we are inscribed and its citizenship.* Homily 12:27

LIFE AFTER INITIATION

In the days after their baptism they heard instructions on the eucharist.

◆◆◆

Theodore knew a preparation and celebration of baptism which emphasized citizenship in the reign of God.

Up through the fifth century the most intense preparation for baptism took place in the weeks preceding it. Although catechumens established some relationship with the community early on, there is little evidence of extensive catechesis or rituals until shortly before initiation. The various ceremonies of the baptismal rite, based on imagery as old as the New Testament, had become more elaborate and not quite uniform. Some postbaptismal formation regularly took place.

Preparation for Baptism

- Those seeking baptism submitted their names near the beginning of Lent. Godparents testified to their character. The names of both groups were inscribed.

- Those to be baptized received instructions about the nature and significance of the preparatory and baptismal rites.

- They underwent exorcisms.

- The Creed was presented to them, and they returned it in the presence of the bishop.

- Those to be baptized renounced Satan, professed faith in Christ and received an anointing on the forehead. Godparents placed a cloth on their heads.

Baptism

- Those to be baptized removed their clothing and received an anointing over their entire bodies.

- The bishop blessed the water.

- He took those to be baptized into the water, placed his hand on their head and immersed them three times in the name of the Trinity.

- The ones being baptized bowed their heads in assent.

- Coming up from the font, they were each given a white garment.

- The bishop sealed them on the forehead in the name of the Trinity.

- They participated in the eucharist with the community.

Life after Initiation

- The baptized received instruction on the eucharist in the days after their initiation.

Pseudo-Dionysius the Areopagite ◆ 16
Mystic and Visionary

He authored a book about the names of God, but his own name is unknown. The obscurity of his identity belies the extent of his influence throughout the church East and West. His mystical theology envisioned a structured reality in which the believer ascended to purification and unity with God. He wrote under a pseudonym, Dionysius the Areopagite.

Silver spoon for
communion, Hama,
Syria, sixth century.

The original Dionysius appeared in the Acts of the Apostles (17:34) as a disciple of Paul. The author who borrowed his name relied on the work of the philosopher Proclus (+ 485) and was quoted by Severus of Antioch (c. 512–518). He was most likely, therefore, a Syrian who wrote his meditations around the turn of the sixth century.

The Ecclesiastical Hierarchy explained the structure of the visible church, a companion to *The Celestial Hierarchy,* a work about the rankings of heavenly beings. *The Ecclesiastical Hierarchy* comprises seven chapters: introduction, baptism, eucharist, the consecration of oil, the clerical hierarchy, the lay hierarchy and funerals. Information about the baptismal ritual of early sixth-century Syria and its meaning is found primarily in the second chapter.

FIRST INTEREST

Pseudo-Dionysius says that what first moves a person toward baptism is "love of transcendent reality and longing for a sacred share of it" (2:2, 2). The goal of baptism was not just entrance into a community, but deeper participation in union with God.

In pursuit of that transcendent goal, the seeker approached a person who was already initiated, asked to be brought to the bishop and promised to obey whatever was necessary. This sponsor or godparent, moved by the desire to assist the other's salvation, took charge of the training and preparation for baptism (2:2, 2). Godparents helped prepare their catechumens for the responses they would make when the time of baptism arrived (2:2, 5).

CATECHESIS

The principal formation for catechumens was the proclamation of the scriptures. Together with those considered possessed and with the penitents among the faithful, catechumens attended the first part of the Divine Liturgy, where they received instructions and heard the singing of the psalms and the reading of the scriptures (3:2). Pseudo-Dionysius says deacons offered catechumens instruction and formation in the scriptures, but it is unclear whether he means in the liturgical setting or at a separate event (6:1, 1). Catechumens did not remain with the faithful for the eucharist, but received only the nourishment of the scriptures during their "incubation" to prepare them for new birth and participation in the church's mysteries (3:3, 6–7; 4:3, 3). "Catechumens, the possessed and penitents should follow the instructions of the holy hierarchy and listen to the singing of the psalms and to the reading of the divinely inspired writings. They may not join in the ensuing sacred acts" (3:3, 6).

With the help of those already initiated, catechumens gradually advanced in self-awareness toward a high state (2:3, 4). They were ready for baptism when they were "filled with the love of God" (2:2, 5).

BAPTISM

Pseudo-Dionysius next explains the extended baptismal rite. He does not say if baptism was preceded by several weeks of instruction, asceticism or liturgical rites,

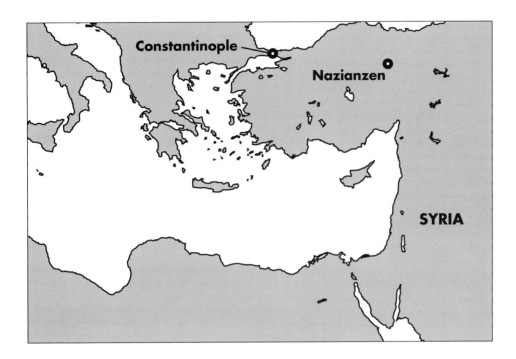

as evidenced so often in the preceding centuries. He does not even refer to a time of year. It appears that baptism was no longer attached to Easter, and preparation no longer coincided with Lent. Formation may have consisted only in the common participation of the liturgy of the word and the personal direction given by the godparent.

At some point, the godparent and the catechumen approached the bishop, who retained a significant role in initiation. The bishop (or "hierarch") rejoiced in their arrival like the shepherd who lifted the lost sheep on his shoulders (Luke 15:5). He prostrated himself and thanked God (2:2, 3). He summoned the clergy to the church for the celebration, which occurred in the context of a eucharist. All sang a hymn of praise, the bishop kissed the altar and then asked the catechumen why he or she had come (2:2, 4).

Repudiating ignorance of God and godless behavior, the one seeking baptism asked the bishop's help to encounter God. The bishop delivered an instruction on the demands of the God-possessed life and asked if the one before him wished to accept it totally. He or she answered yes. The bishop then imposed his hand upon the person's head and marked it with the sign of the cross. The priests enrolled both the catechumen and the sponsor in the holy register as a sign that God was granting a share in the divine life to one who reverently sought it (2:2, 5 and 2:3, 4).

The preparation continued. All joined in a prayer led by the bishop. The catechumen's shoes and outer garments were removed. The catechumen, having been turned west by the deacons, lifted hands in rejection and three times renounced Satan by repeating the words after the bishop and blowing. Next, having been turned east, the catechumen, with eyes raised and hands lifted, accepted

> **The candle that you will light symbolizes the mystery of the luminous procession which will lead you to meet the bridegroom with shining and virginal souls. The light of our candle will be our faith.** Gregory of Nazianzen, *Prayer 45*

the bishop's invitation to submit to Christ by professing faith three times (2:2, 6–7 and 2:3, 5). The bishop placed his hands upon the catechumen, who was now completely stripped by the deacons. The bishop then administered a threefold anointing, and the priests fully covered the catechumen's body with oil to prepare for the combat between good and evil in the baptismal waters (2:2,7 and 2:3,6).

Baptism followed. The bishop consecrated the water and poured chrism into it three times in the form of a cross. He ordered the catechumen to be brought to him. A priest called out the names of the catechumen and godparent, and other priests brought them to the water. The bishop immersed the catechumen thrice, invoking the Trinity; each time, the priests called out the initiate's name. The priests and the godparent reclothed the initiate, who was presented again to the bishop. The bishop anointed the newly baptized with the sign of the cross and proclaimed him or her ready to participate in the eucharist, which all then shared (2:2, 7 and 2:3, 8).

> **When the bishop admits children to a share in the sacred symbols it is so that they may derive nourishment from this and spend their entire lives in the unceasing contemplation of divine things.**
>
> *The Ecclesiastical Hierarchy 7:3, 11*

Pseudo-Dionysius says nothing of a baptismal candle, even though the custom had begun in his region. Gregory of Nazianzen (+ 390) linked it to the garment as a sign of participation in the celestial nuptial banquet *(Prayer 45 on Holy Baptism)*. Proclus of Constantinople (bishop, 434–446) said, "The illumination of your soul is symbolized by the candle that you hold in your hands" *(Homily* 9:49–51).

All this concerned adults, but Pseudo-Dionysius also defended the baptism of children over some objections. He expected parents to entrust children to a good Christian teacher and godparent. The bishop asked such teachers, presumably at the baptism, to pronounce the renunciation and promises, when children would be signed and enrolled (7:3,11).

A child's godparent acted as instructor after baptism; an adult's godparent did so before.

◆◆◆

The catechumenate had assumed a different shape at this time. The time before baptism had been simplified to participation in the word service and the engagement of a godparent. The enrollment, renunciation and exorcistic anointings all took place at baptism. The frequency of infant baptisms caused the custom to come into question.

First Interest

- The desire to share in transcendence first motivated people to seek baptism.

- Those who sought baptism presented themselves to initiated members of the community to obtain their service as a godparent.

Catechesis

- Godparents offered personal instruction.

- Catechumens attended the word service with the faithful and heard instruction on the scriptures.

- They were ready for baptism when they were filled with the love of God.

Baptism

- Baptism took place at the eucharist, but not necessarily at Easter.

- Godparents presented catechumens to the bishop.

- The bishop asked why the catechumens had come. He explained the demands of the Christian life and asked the catechumens if they would accept them.

- The bishop imposed hands on them and signed their forehead.

- He asked the priests to enroll their names.

- Catechumens renounced Satan and accepted Christ, then received handlaying and an anointing.

- The bishop consecrated the water with chrism.

- The bishop immersed the catechumens three times, baptizing them in the name of the Trinity.

- They were clothed and then signed with chrism.

- Although Pseudo-Dionysius does not mention the baptismal candle, it had been introduced into the baptismal liturgy in neighboring regions by this time.

- All joined in the eucharist.

Life after Initiation

- The newly baptized continued their ascent toward spiritual perfection.

17 ◆ John the Deacon
Cleric and Correspondent

Nothing for certain is known about Senarius of Ravenna except that he wrote a letter to John the Deacon. Nothing for certain is known about John the Deacon except that he replied to Senarius of Ravenna. Scholars date the work to the turn of the sixth century. Some believe this John went on to become Pope John I (523–526).

Ruins of the sixth-century baptistry of Aquiléia in Grado, Italy. H. Leclercq, "Baptistére," in *Dictionnaire d'Archeologie et de Liturgie*, vol. 2, Paris: Letouzey et Ané, 1907.

John's letter, incomplete in available manuscripts, answers a series of questions posed by Senarius about church life, including the customs of baptism. The responses give a picture of baptismal preparation and celebration in early sixth-century Rome. John arranged the material according to the questions and not according to an independent, coherent exposition of baptism, so the contemporary reader often wishes to know more.

Those recently exorcised, who had renounced the traps and empty promises of the devil, now deserve to receive the words of the Creed handed down from the apostles. In this way those who a little while ago were only called "catechumens" now may also be called "those petitioning" or "the elect." *Letter to Senarius 4*

Some of Senarius' questions are rather basic, such as, "What is a catechumen?" and "What is catechesis?" They suggest that the intensity of catechumenal preparation known in previous centuries was diminishing in Ravenna.

FIRST INTEREST

John believed the catechumenate was necessary because before baptism one is "restrained by the power of the devil." The catechumenate, then, performed an exorcistic function (3).

CATECHESIS

Before baptism one had to go into the room of the catechumens. *Catechesis,* John says, is the Greek word for *instruction.* "Instruction," he says, is the blessing of handlaying by the minister of the church (3). It is striking that after several centuries in which instruction required at least several weeks of daily exhortations and perhaps as many as several years of reflection on the scriptures, John reports

© 1989 Loyola University Chicago Archives: R.V. Schoder, SJ, photographer.

Arian baptistry mosaic. Ravenna, sixth century.

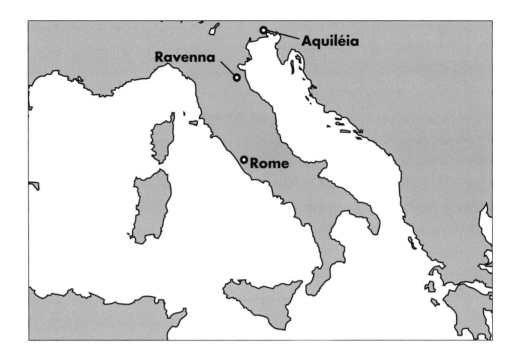

that in sixth-century Rome instruction had been transformed into handlaying and blessing.

Exorcisms by exsufflation accompanied this stage. Someone blew (or hissed?) upon the catechumens to make the devil flee and to raise them up from darkness into the glory of God's love (3).

The catechumens also were signed with blessed salt, indicating the preservative powers of wisdom and preaching. The handlaying which accompanied this invoked the Trinity (3). These catechumenate rituals, salt (witnessed previously by Augustine) and handlaying, perdured even though no instruction accompanied them. John did not directly answer Senarius about the origin of the catechumenate; he just reported the elements of its celebration.

PREPARATION FOR BAPTISM

John says that catechumens entered another stage of preparation during which they became known as "those petitioning" (*competentes*) or "the elect" (*electi*), terms already in use for those preparing for baptism from the time of Ambrose, but now applied to a second stage. He does not indicate how long these periods lasted, but says that the elect were known as catechumens "a little while ago." The new title was assigned when the catechumens renounced the devil and received the Creed (4), two traditional rites still in place in the development of baptismal preparation.

Before people receive baptism, why do they become catechumens? What does "catechumen" mean? "Catechesis"? By what precept was it foreshadowed in the Old Testament? Or is it a new precept that receives more support from the New Testament? Also, what is a scrutiny and why are infants scrutinized three times before Easter? And what does the expectation and purpose of a scrutiny accomplish? And so forth. *Senarius to John the Deacon*

A series of three scrutinies, evident from the letter of Senarius, had already been attested in Rome in the *Canons to the Gauls* (c. 400). John says the scrutinies intended to examine whether the exorcisms had taken effect. Having renounced the devil, had the sacred words (of the Creed) been carved on the hearts of the elect? Did they acknowledge the future grace of redemption? Did they confess to believe in God the Father almighty? If the elect passed this screening favorably, they were anointed with the oil of sanctification on their ears and nostrils. This appears to have developed from the ephpheta rite, but John specifies that the oil was intended to form a wall for the ears to keep out whatever might poison the elect and to permit them to admit the faith which leads to understanding (4). The blessing of the nostrils admonished catechumens to persevere in the service of God and the commandments as long as they drew the breath of life (5). John's scrutiny resembles an interrogation concerning knowledge and sincerity in a ritual which followed exorcisms, rather than one which incorporated them.

BAPTISM

Baptism took place at the Easter Vigil, according to both Senarius' question about scrutinies and John's treatment of the communion rite (12).

The baptismal ceremony included several steps. The elect were anointed on the breast (6), that dwelling place of the heart, with the intent to strengthen their commitment to the commands of Christ. They removed their shoes and clothing to

Image courtesy The Newberry Library, Chicago.

Baptistry in catacombs of Pontian, Rome, sixth century. H. Leclercq, "Baptistére," in *Dictionnaire d'Archeologie et de Liturgie*, vol. 2, Paris: Letouzey et Ané, 1907.

help them accept this spiritual journey undistracted. They were immersed three times in water in the name of the Trinity, recalling the three days Christ spent in the tomb. They were anointed on the head with chrism as priests and royalty. Their heads were covered with a veil, another priestly symbol. They were wrapped in white garments, representing the transfiguration of Jesus and preparing them for the heavenly wedding banquet. The postbaptismal rites signified eternal life in Christ; the anointing and head veil did not pertain specifically to the Holy Spirit.

The newly baptized received a mixture of milk and honey during the communion rite at the Easter Vigil, symbolizing their entrance into the Promised Land: "The new Promised Land is the land of the resurrection and of the one remaining forever in that happiness" (*Letter to Senarius* 12). They became sharers in the body and blood of the Lord.

John clarifies that these rites pertained to infants as well as adults. Infants, sponsored by their parents or by others, were baptized because of someone else's profession of faith (7). An abundance of infant baptisms would explain the change in what constituted catechesis from formal instruction to the blessing of hand-laying. It may also account for the brief time implied for catechumens to become elect. Furthermore, although his letter seems influenced by the *Apostolic Tradition*, it assigns no special role to the bishop in the postbaptismal rituals. All this indicates the primary situation for baptism was shifting from adults at cathedrals to infants in parishes. The catechumenate was adjusting accordingly.

◆◆◆

First Interest

- People sought baptism to be freed from the power of the devil.

- Parents also brought children to be baptized.

Catechesis

- Catechesis consisted in the blessing of handlaying.

- Catechumens were exorcised with exsufflation and were signed with salt.

Preparation for Baptism

- Catechumens became known as "those petitioning" or "the elect" when they renounced Satan and received the Creed.

- Three scrutinies, during which the elect were anointed on their ears and nostrils, examined the sincerity of their conversion and their knowledge of the Creed.

Baptism

- Baptism took place during the Easter Vigil.

- These rites pertained to infants as well as to adults.

- The elect received an anointing on the breast and removed their clothing.

- They were immersed three times in water in the name of the Trinity.

- They were anointed on the head with chrism.

- They received a head covering and white clothing.

- They participated in the eucharist, also receiving a cup of milk and honey.

Caesarius of Arles ◆ 18
Captive and Convener

A preacher known for fifteen-minute homilies, who used examples from daily life and whined about people's lack of participation, Caesarius (c. 470–543) served as bishop of Arles for the last forty years of his life. In the midst of turbulent political times Caesarius' devotion to his work did not protect him from enemies who twice exiled him on suspicion of treason. King Theodoric exonerated him at trial in Ravenna, and Caesarius resumed a vigorous ministry. He convened and took part in a number of councils in Gaul that helped bring order to the church's leadership and ministry.

Cliché Arch. Photo © CNMHS, Paris.

Baptism of Clovis, King of the Franks, 496. Detail of tapestry at Reims.

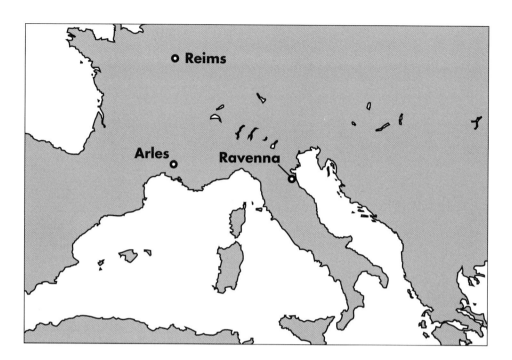

The service of baptism took on special significance because Clovis, the king of the Franks, had been baptized just a few years before Caesarius became bishop. With the king came countless Franks for Christian formation and baptism. Caesarius addressed them in several sermons. These offer excellent evidence for baptismal customs in sixth-century Gaul.

PREPARATION FOR BAPTISM

Caesarius preferred that baptism be celebrated according to "the legitimate order." For unbaptized children, this meant arriving at church with parents at the beginning of Lent, participation in several vigils during the season, and baptism at Easter (*Sermon* 84:6). Parents fasted on behalf of the children, who received anointings and handlayings from the minister. Caesarius signed catechumens on the forehead that the devil might leave them (*Sermon* 121:8); however, he says nothing about scrutinies with their intense exorcisms. Although in previous centuries a bishop addressed his prebaptismal instructions primarily to adult catechumens, Caesarius addressed his homilies to parents; a large number of candidates for baptism were children.

When Christians are immersed three times in the saving bath, as by a journey of three days, the spiritual Egyptians (that is, original sins and actual offenses) are buried, so to speak, in the Red Sea. As the children of Israel cross into the service of God, only their sins suffer drowning. *Sermon* 97:1

Caesarius made some exceptions within this legitimate order for children. If parents missed the opportunity for baptism at Easter, they could present their children on another feast day. The preparation could even be shortened: Parents could present their children a week before baptism; they could observe fasting and vigils at that time (*Sermon* 229:6), and children could receive anointings and handlaying (*Sermon* 225:6).

Some requesting baptism were adults. Caesarius called them *competentes,* or "those petitioning." He rarely used the term *catechumen.* He expected them to submit their names for baptism several days before Easter, apparently an informal procedure. At that time they received anointing and hand-laying (*Sermon* 200:2).

Caesarius interpreted adult baptism as a victory over the power of the devil; it freed people from sin and enabled them to do good works and to desire eternal rewards (*Sermon* 200:2). Consequently, its preparation required ritual support and behavioral change. During this period those who were "vessels of the devil" became "vessels of Christ." Caesarius expected the petitioners to improve their behavior: to banish hatred against others; to offer and seek forgiveness; to restore stolen goods; to repent of theft, murder, adultery and abortion; to resist envy; to abhor lies; to avoid drunkenness; to eat and drink properly; to shun injustice; and to be kind, humble, mild and temperate (*Sermon* 200:3–5).

Caesarius presented the Creed to all those preparing for baptism, children as well as adults, sometime during Lent, in order that they might recite it back. All in the community were expected to memorize the Creed. The Council of Agde, over which he presided in 506, established the Sunday before Easter as the regional day for this presentation (canon 13). Caesarius delivered a sermon later titled "Reproof Needing to Be Read to the People at the Presentation of the Creed" (*Sermon* 201) on such an occasion, but that sermon does not allude to the rite. In that sermon, he asked the community to teach it to those preparing for baptism so that those who were old enough could return it themselves, while godparents or someone representing them could return it for the children (*Sermon* 13:2; 130:5).

Godparents assisted in other ways. Caesarius called them *fideiussores* or "those testifying to faithfulness." (A godparent was called *compater* or "co-parent" for the first time at a council in Auxerre in 578.) Such people were expected to teach not only the Creed but also the Lord's Prayer to children (*Sermon* 13:2). Caesarius asked godparents to give good example before and after baptism (*Sermon* 200:6).

I ask you, brothers and sisters, if you want your child or servant baptized, do not delay to bring them even now to the church. It is not right that something believed to be so great and splendid is sought negligently or later than appropriate. For I fear that some women will not bring their infants later, since they neglect to come to the vigils with them. For most certainly we believe that, when Lent is just beginning, those who want to bring the ones needing baptism will still come with them faithfully to the vigils, and their children will receive the sacrament of baptism according to the legitimate order, and they will acquire an indulgence of sins. *Sermon 84:6*

Modern-day Arles, France.

It is good and legitimate that those who are well wait for the Easter solemnity, and that they fast and keep vigil on the days of Lent according to church law, and that they approach the oil or the impositions of the hand. But it is right that those who want their child to be baptized on some other festival come instead to church with the child seven days before and fast and keep vigil there, or you have your child approach the oil or the imposition of the hand, as has been said before, and so receive the sacraments of baptism according to the legitimate order. *Sermon* 229:6

Although he distinguished "those who receive sons and daughters with pious love" from parents (*Sermon* 13:2), Caesarius sometimes addressed godparents, parents and the entire community as *fideiussores*.

BAPTISM

Several rituals took place at baptism. The bishop asked those to be baptized to renounce the devil, his empty promises and works. Parents answered for infants (*Sermon* 12:3; cf. *Sermons* 173:3 and 200:6). Because he viewed baptism as a break in the devil's power, Caesarius stressed the renunciation, not one's confession of belief in Christ. He baptized with a triple immersion in the name of the Trinity (*Sermon* 124:4) in imitation of ancient Israel's three-day journey to the Red Sea (*Sermon* 97:1). He called the newly baptized "infants," no matter their age (*Sermon* 129:5; 205:2), or "neophytes" (see, for example, 201:1).

Caesarius noted several postbaptismal rituals. As with the prebaptismal data, this information appears piecemeal in a variety of homilies; their sequence cannot be certainly established. The newly baptized received chrism and the oil of blessing that they might be filled with God and become temples of God (*Sermon* 128:2). They were clothed in white (*Sermon* 201:2). They probably participated in the eucharist: Caesarius noted (*Sermon* 161:1) that the Good Samaritan poured a mixture of oil and wine into the victim's wounds (Luke 10:34). "Certainly in the oil is the anointing of chrism; in the wine the consecration of the eucharist." This might imply a baptismal eucharist. The feet of the baptized were washed (*Sermon* 204:3), and they promised in turn to wash the feet of guests (*Sermon* 64:2). Baptism entitled Christians to exchange the kiss of peace (*Sermon* 88:1).

LIFE AFTER INITIATION

After the baptism of children, godparents were expected to continue setting a good example so children might grow in Christian behavior. "Godparents should admonish, reprimand, and correct godchildren that they might observe justice, guard chastity, maintain virginity until marriage, refrain their tongue from cursing or from lying, not offer dirty or sensual songs from their mouth, not be proud, and not be envious. They should not hold anger or hatred in their heart. They should not follow fortune tellers nor hang amulets or satanic signs on themselves or others. They should flee from magicians and other ministers of the devil. They should keep the catholic faith, go more frequently to church, and hear the sacred readings with attentive ears, not with unruly talking. They should receive pilgrims and wash their feet according to what was done for them at baptism. They should themselves keep peace and strive to call the discordant back to harmony. They should bestow honor and the love of true charity onto the priests and their parents" (*Sermon* 204:3; see also *Sermons* 13:2; 50:3, 130:5; 200:6; 229:6).

◆◆◆

Caesarius served a church with a growing number of infant baptisms, which called for pastoral adaptations of the catechumenate and baptism.

Preparation for Baptism

- Adults seeking baptism submitted their names shortly before Easter.

- Parents seeking baptism for their children presented them at church near the beginning of Lent.

- During Lent those to be baptized fasted and participated in vigils. Parents did so on behalf of their children.

- Those to be baptized received anointings, signations on the forehead and handlaying.

- Adults were expected to improve their behavior before baptism, indicating their freedom from the devil.

- Godparents assisted in instruction of the Creed and the Lord's Prayer, and by their example.

- The bishop presented the Creed to those to be baptized, and they were expected to return it. Godparents or substitutes for them returned the Creed for young children.

- This preparation could be abbreviated.

Baptism

- Baptism normally took place at Easter but could be celebrated on other feasts.

- Those to be baptized renounced the devil. Parents answered for their children.

- Baptism was administered by a triple immersion in the name of the Trinity.

- The newly baptized were anointed with chrism.

- They were clothed in white.

- They may have shared the eucharist.

- Their feet were washed.

- They were entitled to the kiss of peace.

Life after Initiation

- The newly baptized were expected to live a moral life.

- Godparents were expected to continue the moral formation of the children they sponsored.

The Gelasian
Sacramentary
Prayer and Ritual

Around the year 750, if the scholarly theory is correct, a convent of religious women in Chelles, near Paris, transcribed the most influential liturgical book of their day. Those who labored on the manuscript copied an older work, now lost. It probably originated a century or two earlier in Rome as a simple collection of rituals, but was embellished as it passed into Gaul. The expanded book gathered the evidence of developing liturgical patterns, whether or not their forms were still in use. The work, which concentrated on prayer texts rather than on rubrics, was called a *sacramentary*, the first of its kind.

Image courtesy The Newberry Library, Chicago.

Sketch of the baptistry of Riez, sixth to eighth century. H. Leclercq, "Baptistère," in *Dictionnaire d'Archeologie chrétienne et de Liturgie*, vol. 2, Paris: Letouzey et Ané, 1907.

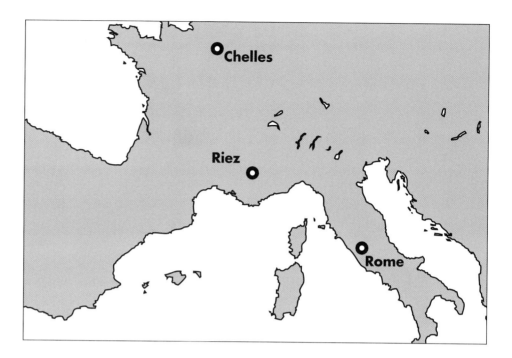

The manuscript from Chelles, now in the Vatican, is the oldest extant example of this much-copied work. Its usage throughout western Europe contributed to the unification of the church's rites as no previous work ever had. For a while its authorship was erroneously attributed to the fifth-century Pope Gelasius I, whose name remained attached to the work under its popular title, the *Gelasian Sacramentary*.

Luke the evangelist bears the image of an ox, in whose place our savior was slain. For this gospel, preparing to speak in this way of Christ, begins with Zachary and Elizabeth, from whom John the Baptist was born in their great old age. What is born soft reaches fullest hardness. Therefore, Luke may be compared to an ox because it has two horns, the two testaments, and four hooves on its feet, the four gospels. *Gelasian Sacramentary 34*

In practice, the catechesis and liturgies of the catechumenate had become quite simplified in parishes; however, the unused liturgical texts survived in books. The *Gelasian* contained texts concerning baptism that originated primarily from Rome, but they had accrued several layers of traditions, some ancient, some contemporary. Not all the parts fit together into one coherent ritual. The catechumenate texts, therefore, are not one continuous series of rites; they are, rather, a compilation of many simpler, but not always compatible, traditions.

The baptismal texts in the *Gelasian Sacramentary* probably come from at least three different periods of history. The earliest could date from the sixth century, if not earlier. The next group of texts drew from a seventh-century document called *Ordo XI*. A third group probably adapted to the eighth-century need for prayers at infant baptism.

The texts from *Ordo XI* provided a significant contribution. Between the seventh and the tenth centuries much liturgical information was passed on in *orders*, texts that described how the rituals were to unfold. Orders of liturgical events were compiled regionally and numbered in later centuries for the sake of identification. *Ordo XI*, one of the earliest, came from late sixth- or early seventh-century Rome.

So when the convent at Chelles produced its version of the *Gelasian* in the eighth century, the compilers included some texts from the well-known seventh-century *Ordo XI*, some that were even older than that and some that were newer.

These and other liturgical documents of the period demonstrate two tensions in the catechumenate: the preservation of its original forms and the adaptations for contemporary needs.

> **I sign you in the name of the Father and of the Son and of the Holy Spirit, that you may be a Christian: your eyes, that you may see the brightness of God; your ears, that you may hear the voice of the Lord; your nostrils, for the sweetness of the odor of Christ; your tongue, that as a convert you may confess the Father and the Son and the Holy Spirit; your heart, that you may believe the inseparable Trinity. Peace be with you, through Jesus Christ our Lord who lives with the Father and the Holy Spirit.** *Gothic Missal 32:254*

PREPARATION FOR BAPTISM

Since the *Gelasian Sacramentary* is primarily a collection of prayers recited by the presider at public worship, it does not tell how to join a catechumenate or how to catechize. Furthermore, many texts respond to a particular pastoral situation, the baptism of infants. Consequently the *Gelasian* includes abbreviated catechumenal texts presuming a shortened baptismal preparation.

This sacramentary presents for the first time a complete order for making an unbaptized adult a catechumen (71). The compiler preserved an old text that was rarely used by the eighth century. The order instructs the presbyter to catechize the unbaptized with inspiring words and exhort them to a moral life after they recognize Christian truth. Then the presbyter blew on their faces (an exorcistic act) and made the sign of the cross on their foreheads. He imposed a hand on their heads and prayed that they would turn from idols and worship the Trinity. They tasted "the medicine of salt" and signed themselves. Then the presbyter prayed again for their progress toward baptism. The *Gelasian* does not designate a time of year for this.

Another document, the *Gothic Missal* from the late seventh or early eighth century, describes a more extensive signation in the "Order for Making a Christian." It contains a prayer for the signation of the eyes, ears, nostrils, tongue and heart.

Overall, the prayers for baptismal preparation and baptism in the *Gelasian* are grouped during the seasons of Lent and Easter. The entire sacramentary is arranged according to the liturgical year. The *Gelasian* proposed baptism at Easter and viewed Lent as a time of preparation for infants and godparents. Even so, the procedures described represent different strands of tradition and do not completely integrate into one.

For example, the *Gelasian* gives a set of prayers for scrutiny Masses (26–28). They include the prayers offered by the presider at the opening of Mass, over the gifts, during the eucharistic prayer, at communion and in blessing the people. They are clearly marked for the third, fourth and fifth Sundays of a six-week Lent. The opening prayers requested the rebirth of the elect. The presider was directed to pause during the eucharistic prayer so that someone could read the names of the

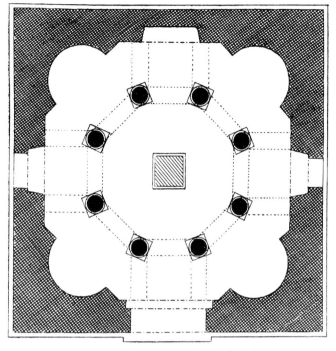

Image courtesy The Newberry Library, Chicago.

Floor plan of the baptistry of Riez, sixth to eighth century. H. Leclercq, "Baptistère," in *Dictionnaire d'Archeologie chrétienne et de Liturgie*, vol. 2, Paris: Letouzey et Ané, 1907.

godparents and the elect. This section says nothing more, however, about the scrutiny itself nor about the inscription of names, which must have preceded. There is no evidence of a dismissal, which would have been impractical for infants anyway. These prayers probably represent an ancient stratum of Roman tradition from at least the early sixth century.

Next, however, the *Gelasian* proposes a collection of prayers for catechumens that presumes a later tradition (29). The scrutiny texts are given in great detail, but they are specified for a weekday to be chosen from the third week of Lent at noon. A public announcement on Monday invited the people to the liturgical event the next day. The presider is a presbyter (see, for example, 29) and the catechumens are infants (for example, 35). Various rites string out at this point; it is not clear whether they were performed all at once or on several occasions. Instructions for Palm Sunday follow this section, suggesting that, however the rituals were done, they were completed by then.

These rites unfold in several steps. The acolyte wrote down the names of the infants when they arrived at the church. He then called out the names. The boys were arranged on the right, girls on the left. The presbyter then offered a prayer "over the elect to make them catechumens"

Therefore we ask, Lord, that you may be pleased to accept this offering not only of our service, but also of all your family, which we offer to you also for those whom you have deigned to give rebirth out of water and the Holy Spirit, granting them forgiveness of all their sins, that you may find them in Christ Jesus our Lord. *Gelasian Sacramentary 45*

(30). In the *Gelasian*, the inscription of names identified the elect, who were then made catechumens for baptism. The prayer must have originated from a time when those to be made catechumens were adults starting a time of learning and moral formation: "Look upon your servants whom you have deigned to call to the beginnings of faith. . . . May they progress from day to day that they may be made worthy to arrive at the grace of the received healing of your baptism."

Next, the presbyter exorcised the salt and prayed that God would make it effective for salvation and exorcism. "After this prayer you place salt in the mouth of the infant and say, 'N., receive the salt of wisdom. May it bring benefits for eternal life'" (31). He then said another prayer (32).

Then the elect were exorcised (33). The acolyte imposed a hand upon them while the presbyter began a series of prayers. The first addressed the God of Abraham, Isaac and Jacob, who led Moses, appeared on Sinai and brought Israel from Egypt by an angel; it asked God to send a holy angel to protect the elect and lead them to the grace of baptism. Then the presbyter addressed the devil to leave those whom Jesus had called to baptism. The presbyter signed the foreheads of the elect. Then he prayed over the girls that the God of all the living would lead them to baptism. He then repeated the same rebuke of the devil and the signation. More prayers followed in a similar pattern: over the boys, over the girls, and then a rebuke of the devil with signation. The priest concluded with a prayer that God would enlighten the intelligence of the elect: "May they keep firm hope, right counsel, and holy doctrine, that they may be fit to receive your grace." Formerly, exorcisms concluded when the candidates for baptism renounced Satan and confessed their faith in God, but the *Gelasian*, which was dealing with infants here, stopped after the prayers of the priest. Although the *Gelasian* neglects the catechetical component of the catechumenate, the content of these prayers may have taught people about the power of God.

The next ritual was an innovation: a presentation of the gospels "for opening the ears of the elect" (34). Similar to the presentation of the Creed and the Lord's Prayer which follow it, the presentation of the gospels constituted a formal prebaptismal ritual. The *Gelasian's* title, however, recalls the one Ambrose assigned to the ephphetha: the "mystery of the opening." Four deacons processed from the sacristy carrying four books, each containing one gospel, accompanied by two candles and incense. The gospels were placed on the four corners of the altar. The presbyter explained the significance of the gospels. A deacon asked all to be silent and listen, and the beginning of Matthew's gospel was read. After the opening verses the presbyter explained Matthew's symbol, a human being. The deacon asked for silence as the opening of Mark's gospel was read. The presbyter explained Mark's symbol, the lion. And so on through the ox for Luke and the eagle for John. The ritual must have been impressive but extravagant for infant catechumens. Still, the community would have benefited from its catechesis.

Next came the presentation of the Creed (35). It also began with the presbyter's explanatory instruction. The acolyte lifted up a child, held the infant in his left arm and placed his right hand upon the child's head. The presbyter asked in which language the family confessed Jesus Christ the Lord. The acolyte responded, "Greek." The presbyter asked him to announce the faith of believers. The acolyte, hand upon the child's head, recited the Creed in Greek, a task once performed by the assembly. The same steps followed for those who spoke Latin. The presbyter concluded with another explanation.

A third presentation followed, that of the Lord's Prayer (36). The deacon asked for everyone's attention. The presbyter introduced the ritual, again with an explanation, then proclaimed the meaning of the Lord's Prayer, phrase by phrase. The deacon asked for attention yet again, and the presbyter

From Herbert Norris, *Church Vestments: Their Origin and Development.* London: Orion, 1949.

Sketch of an eighth-century papal tiara.

urged all to reflect on these words. Surely the adults in the assembly benefited more than the infants.

These rituals, from the scrutiny on the third Tuesday of Lent up to this point, appear one after the other in the *Gelasian* between the texts for Mass on Saturday of the fifth week and those for Palm Sunday. *Ordo XI* contains a fuller explanation of these rites. The compiler of the *Gelasian* probably inserted these newer texts into an older tradition after they had become popular from the circulation of *Ordo XI*.

O God, deign to hear your servants, who bow their heads to you. May they come to the font of washing, so that, those who were created in your likeness, reborn by water and the Holy Spirit, having removed the old person, may put on the new. *Gelasian Sacramentary* 71

In *Ordo XI* the rites of baptismal preparation took place over a period of seven occasions, to symbolize the seven gifts of the Holy Spirit (81); all seven occasions were called *scrutinies.*

Ordo XI's first scrutiny, on Wednesday of the third week of Lent, contained the inscription of names, the signation on the forehead (here done by the godparents, since infants could not do it themselves), the imposition of hands, the salt ritual, a dismissal, a return to the assembly and exorcisms with signations over the boys and girls. Catechumens were then dismissed, and parents and godparents participated in the Mass on their behalf (1–37).

All returned on Saturday that week for the second scrutiny, which repeated only the exorcisms and signations from the first meeting (38–39).

The third occasion, Wednesday of the fourth week, began with the exorcisms and signations, and then added the rite "for the opening of the ears," the presentation of the four gospels. The presentation of the Creed and of the Lord's Prayer, virtually as described in the *Gelasian*, followed immediately (40–76).

All returned twice during the fifth week and once early in the sixth week, on days the presbyter would announce, to repeat the simpler ritual of the second meeting (77–82). The seventh scrutiny took place on Holy Saturday morning (83–88), as in the *Gelasian*.

By this time the *Würzburg Evangelary* (c. 645), a collection of gospels for Mass in Rome, called for the reading of the story of the woman at the well (John 4:6–42) on Friday of the third week of Lent, the man born blind (John 9:1–38) on Wednesday of the fourth week and the raising of Lazarus (John 11:1–45) on Friday of the fourth week. These probably evolved from their use at scrutiny rites for catechumens. Although the Ambrosian rite (according to the ninth-century *Bergamo Sacramentary,* probably representing an even earlier tradition) proclaimed these scriptures on the second, fourth and fifth Sundays of Lent, the Roman rite kept them on weekdays.

For the Saturday morning before Easter the *Gelasian* offers prebaptismal rites (42). The presbyter placed a hand upon the infants' heads and offered another exorcism. Then he touched the nostrils and ears of the children with his saliva (no longer with oil, still including the nose, now mimicking Jesus' miracle) while offering an invocation. The presbyter then anointed the children on the breast and "between the shoulders" (no longer the entire body) with exorcised oil. At this point he asked each by name, "Do you renounce Satan? And all his works? And all his empty promises?" "I renounce," came the response. The text appears to presume that the response came from the one to be baptized, but in the case of infants it probably came from the godparents.

The Saturday morning ritual continued with the return of the Creed. Faced again with the inability of infants to participate at this point, the *Gelasian* created a new solution: The presbyter recited the Creed himself while imposing his hand on the infant's head. The archdeacon asked the elect to pray, kneel and say Amen together. They did so. Then he asked the catechumens to leave. The deacon repeated the instructions: "My most dear children, go back to your places and await the hour when God's grace may perform baptism among you."

BAPTISM

Baptism took place at the Easter Vigil, which the *Gelasian* began at 2:30 in the afternoon (42). Opening with the offering of the candle and the blessing of its incense, the liturgy continued with a long series of scripture readings and prayers, all dwelling on the new birth of baptism and Easter. A procession to the font formed and the litany for baptizing was sung (43). The presbyter blessed the font.

Individual baptisms began. The renunciation and anointing had already taken place that morning, so the presbyter proceeded to the profession of faith. "Do you believe in God the Father almighty? And do you believe in Jesus Christ his only Son our Lord, who was born and suffered? And do you believe in the Holy Spirit, the holy church, the forgiveness of sins and the resurrection of the body?" "I believe," came the response each time. Once again, it appears that the response comes from the one to be baptized, but godparents probably replied for infants. An immersion took place after each of the three responses.

> **"Remember, Lord, your servants, the men and women who will receive your elect for the holy grace of your baptism, and all those standing here."** Then be silent. The names of the men and women who will receive those infants are recited.
>
> **"We pray that you might receive this offering, Lord. . . ."** The names of the elect are recited. *Gelasian Sacramentary* 26

Anointings followed baptism. The presbyter anointed the crown of the infant's head with chrism and offered a prayer. Then "the Holy Spirit [was] given by the bishop," who placed his hand on each infant's head and prayed for the sevenfold gift of the Spirit with a text drawn from Ambrose. He signed them on the forehead with chrism, saying, "The sign of Christ for eternal life." "Amen," came the response. "Peace be with you." "And also with you." The *Gelasian* says nothing about the white garment or the baptismal candle. The Mass continued with the "Glory to God" at dusk, "when a star appears in the sky." The presider's prayers at the Mass frequently referred to the newly baptized (see, for example, 45). The entire celebration was offered again on the vigil of Pentecost (66).

LIFE AFTER INITIATION

Infants returned to Mass throughout Easter week. The petition inserted into the eucharistic prayer at the Easter Vigil on their behalf was repeated at Mass daily through the Sunday after Easter (46–53). The *Gelasian* also included a Mass for the anniversary of baptism (54). It invited those baptized at Easter to return the following year in celebration.

◆◆◆

Although the catechumenate and its rites had been developed and reduced, their existence was still prized by the community and celebrated in the midst of the faithful.

Preparation for Baptism

- According to an old order, adults seeking baptism became catechumens in a liturgical event:

    - The presbyter catechized them by exhortation.

    - He blew in their face, signed their forehead with a cross, imposed a hand and prayed for them to give up false worship. The catechumens tasted salt and signed themselves with the cross; the presbyter prayed for their progress.

- An early tradition placed the scrutinies at Mass on the third, fourth and fifth Sundays of Lent.

- A later tradition developed with scrutinies on weekdays of Lent:

    - These began with an inscription of names and the giving of salt. A typical scrutiny then included handlaying, exorcisms and signations, but no longer concluded with renunciation. Godparents signed the foreheads of infants for them.

    - Boys and girls were exorcised separately.

    - The gospels of the woman at the well, the man born blind and the raising of Lazarus appeared on lenten weekdays, probably to accompany scrutinies.

    - Three presentations followed: of the gospels (new to *Ordo XI* and the *Gelasian Sacramentary*), of the Creed (in which the acolyte replaced the assembly), and of the Lord's Prayer. At the rites the presbyter explained their significance.

    - On Holy Saturday morning, those to be baptized experienced handlaying, another exorcism, the ephphetha rite with saliva, anointing on their breast and between the shoulders, and the renunciation of the devil.

    - The presbyter himself recited the Creed for the infants.

Baptism

- Baptism took place at the Easter vigil.

- After the water blessing, those to be baptized were asked to profess their faith in the Trinity. Godparents answered for infants.

- The presbyter baptized each person three times by immersion as the questions were answered.

- The presbyter anointed the newly baptized.

- If the bishop were present he imposed hands, prayed for the sevenfold gift of the Spirit and anointed the newly baptized.

- All shared in the eucharist.

- The ritual was offered again at Pentecost.

Life after Initiation

- The newly baptized participated in the eucharist throughout the octave of Easter.

- They were invited to celebrate again on the anniversary of their baptism.

20 ◆ The Roman-Germanic Pontifical
Access and Unity

In 963, the Roman synod under the leadership of Emperor Otto I deposed Pope John XII, who had been forcefully and illegally elected eight years earlier at age 18 and was accused of selling ordinations, ordaining a ten-year-old bishop, giving sacred vessels to prostitutes and generally turning the Lateran Palace into a brothel. They chose a layman to become Pope Leo VIII. Within two days Leo went through the entire sequence of ordination rites, which were by then conveniently accessible, thanks to a compilation of liturgical texts that became known as the *Roman-Germanic Pontifical.*

From Rev. Wharton B. Marriott, *Vestiarium Christianum: The Origin and Gradual Development of the Dress of Holy Ministry in the Church,* London: Rivingtons, 1868.

A bishop administering chrism, ninth century.

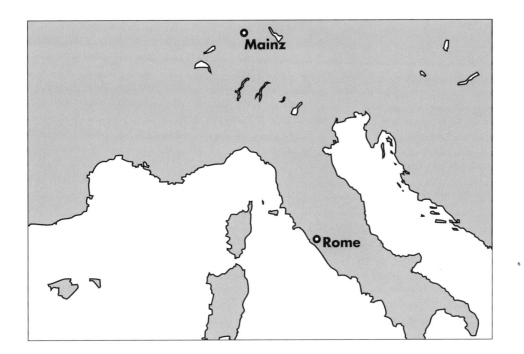

These texts had been gathered from 950 to 962 in St. Alban's monastery in Mainz, where Otto's son William was both protector of the monastery and archbishop of the city. In an effort to bring reform and unity to the liturgy throughout the newly established Holy Roman Empire, Otto promoted and obtained the widespread use of this liturgical book, which collected in one place the proliferating non-eucharistic liturgies over which a bishop presided. Therein may be found the catechumenate as the tenth-century church knew it, in a section also known as *Ordo L*, which incorporated *Ordo XI*.

So many people had grown unfamiliar with the catechumenate that the *Roman-Germanic Pontifical* included a glossary of terms and an explanation of its rituals (111). It gave the Latin equivalents of Greek terms and then answered why one executes each rite.

PREPARATION FOR BAPTISM

At first glance, the order of becoming a catechumen (110) resembles the one from the *Gelasian Sacramentary*. The priest was expected to catechize the individuals and invite them to renounce Satan and to profess their belief in the Trinity. Exorcisms, signations, handlaying and the giving of salt followed, all as in the *Gelasian*. However, the *Gelasian* concludes the rite of becoming a catechumen there, whereas the *Roman-Germanic Pontifical* goes on. It added the lenten exorcisms found in the *Gelasian*, as well as the ephphetha ceremonies of Holy Saturday morning. The same rite still went on: It called for the blessing of the water, the profession of faith in the

> **Next it must be asked what a scrutiny is. It is called a scrutiny from "scrutinizing," because before baptism it is necessary to scrutinize the faith of the catechumen.** *Roman-Germanic Pontifical* 111

Trinity, and then baptism, followed by the presbyteral anointing with chrism and communion—and confirmation if the bishop were present. Thus, instead of presenting the order for becoming a catechumen as a rite separate from the scrutinies

The washing of holy baptism on the body profits nothing, if in the soul the acceptance of the catholic faith by using reason has not preceded. . . . Therefore, infants—not using reason, tainted by the sins of others—may be saved by the faith and confession of others through the sacrament of baptism, if they keep the entirety of the faith confessed for them when the appropriate age arrives. Alcuin, *Letter* 110

and from baptism, the tenth-century *Pontifical* united them all into one ceremony.

This ritual seems to describe how baptism was celebrated on a day other than Easter and Pentecost. A similar ritual appears for the baptism of infants, not connected to Easter (107).

Such rituals did not develop without caution. Alcuin (c. 735–804) believed that religious instruction should accompany baptism. He warned that adults should understand what they were receiving in baptism and that infants should be instructed as they matured (*Letter* 110).

The *Roman-Germanic Pontifical* also preserved the rites for baptism at Easter with preparation during Lent, even though the compilers had placed an entire baptismal rite in the context of "becoming a catechumen." The more extensive order begins with a series of seven scrutinies. The first took place on Wednesday of the third week of Lent around nine in the morning. It resembles the scrutiny from the *Gelasian*. The inscription of names of infants and godparents, renunciations, professions of faith, blowing in the face, exorcisms, giving salt, signations and handlaying took place at a Mass in which the godparents and those to be baptized were remembered by name during the eucharistic prayer (99:85–119). A second, similar scrutiny was celebrated during the fourth week (99:120–125). In the fifth week the third scrutiny added the rites "for opening the ears"—the presentation of the gospels, the Lord's Prayer, and the Creed—with considerable ceremony and explanation (99:126–157). Two more scrutinies were held within a week, and another during the week before Easter (99:158). At the seventh, held on Holy Saturday, "they are catechized [meaning *exorcised*], and they return the Creed and are baptized."

A little earlier, Amalarius of Metz (c. 780–850) had explained that he followed the Roman ritual with its signations, genuflections and exorcisms. He also taught the Lord's Prayer and the Creed to the godmothers and godfathers, who would similarly teach them to those they sponsored (*Letter to Charlemagne on Baptism*, "Scrutiny" 10). He had the godparents return the Creed before baptism ("Renunciation" 40). To Amalarius the ritual was no longer a scrutiny of the catechumen's holiness, but a scrutiny of the godparents' knowledge of the Creed.

The seventh scrutiny found in the *Roman-Germanic Pontifical* is described more fully (99:337–341). At nine on Holy Saturday morning those to be baptized arrived at church with their godparents. Those who were old enough recited the Lord's Prayer and the Creed; godparents did so for infants. The priest signed those to be baptized on the forehead, imposed his hand and exorcised them. He performed the ephphetha rite with his saliva, saying first in the right ear, "Ephphetha, that is, be opened to the aroma of sweetness." (The formula was borrowed from the anointing of nostrils.) Then in the left ear, "But you, devil, flee, for the judgment of God is drawing near." He anointed them, and asked them to renounce Satan. He walked around, imposed a hand on them all and sang the Creed.

BAPTISM

Baptisms took place during the Easter Vigil (99:342–396). The fire ritual, which opened the service, began at one in the afternoon. The reading of the scriptures followed, during which a priest performed the Saturday morning rituals for any infants who had not been in attendance (363). Immediately afterwards, two acolytes appeared holding the vessels for chrism and the oil of catechumens. Standing at the right of the altar, they processed to the font. The choir followed, singing a litany. The bishop joined them to bless the font at about three in the afternoon. After an elaborate blessing, he sprinkled those standing around with water from the font, many of whom then collected water in vessels to take with them to sprinkle in their homes and on their crops (368).

We thoroughly scrutinize the godfathers and godmothers, to see if they can sing the Lord's Prayer and the Creed as we had advised. Amalarius, *Letter to Charlemagne on Baptism,* "Renunciation" 40

For baptisms, the bishop asked the name of each one, and then, in three questions, asked if he or she believed in the persons of the Trinity. Each responded "I believe." He asked, "Do you wish to be baptized?" "I do." He baptized one or two or however many children he wished, immersing them three times while reciting the formula, then returned them to their godparents. Presbyters, deacons and acolytes baptized the rest—boys first, then girls—pointing the infants' head a different direction for each immersion: to the east, to the north, and then to the south (370–371; 376). A presbyter anointed them with chrism while the godparent kept their feet in the water (377–378). They received a white head covering and ten coins, the meaning of which is obscure; the minister then offered them the sign of peace (380).

The newly baptized then arranged themselves for confirmation. Godparents held infants in their right hands; older candidates placed a foot upon the right foot of the godparent. While the archdeacon held the chrism, the bishop imposed a hand over the heads of all and prayed for the sevenfold gift of the Spirit. The deacons asked the names of each while the bishop dipped his thumb in chrism and made the cross on each one's forehead, saying, "I confirm and consign you in the name of the Father and of the Son and of the Holy Spirit." Each responded Amen. They exchanged the greeting of peace. Blessings followed (382–389).

Amidst the ringing of bells and the lighting of the neophytes' candles, Mass was resumed. The newly baptized also received communion, a practice they continued throughout the octave of Easter as their parents brought them to daily Mass (390–396). All this could be repeated at Pentecost (477).

◆◆◆

During the tenth century, two methods of baptism were circulated, an extensive one for baptism by a bishop at Easter or Pentecost, with its preparatory rites during Lent, and a version for other times of the year which collected all the rites into one event.

Preparation for Baptism

- Those to be baptized at Easter participated in seven preparatory ceremonies during Lent, called "scrutinies," which included inscription, renunciation and profession, exsufflation, salt, handlaying, signations, exorcisms and the presentations of the gospels, Creed and Lord's Prayer.

- More rites followed on Holy Saturday morning, including the return of the Lord's Prayer and Creed, signation, handlaying, exorcism, the ephphetha, anointing and renunciation.

Baptism

- Baptism took place at the Easter Vigil.

    - The font was blessed, the profession of faith made, and the candidates were immersed three times in the name of the Trinity.

    - The newly baptized were anointed with chrism and received a head covering and ten coins.

    - The bishop confirmed the newly baptized.

    - They received lighted candles.

    - All participated in the eucharist.

- Another order of service combined many prebaptismal and baptismal rituals into one rite, presumably for children apart from Easter and Pentecost.

Life after Initiation

- Those baptized at Easter and Pentecost returned each day during the octave for Mass and communion.

The Roman Pontifical
Reform and Sobriety

21

T he spirit of reform promoted by Pope Gregory VII (1073–1085) created a new allegiance to the authority of the papacy. In the years following his death various attempts at liturgical reform slowly reshaped the *Roman-Germanic Pontifical* of the tenth century into the *Roman Pontifical* of the twelfth century. The reforms eliminated parts of the older work that seemed to be too "German" and not "Roman" enough, while reintroducing a spirit of sobriety in the liturgy. The *Roman Pontifical's* treatment of the catechumenate and baptism demonstrates these trends.

From Herbert Norris, *Church Vestment: Their Origin and Development*. London: Orion, 1949.

St. Clement at the altar, from an eleventh-century fresco in Rome.

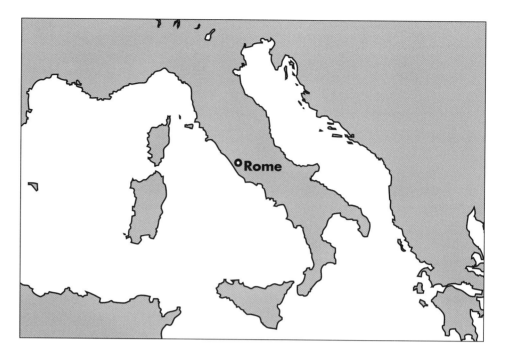

PREPARATION FOR BAPTISM

In the history of the catechumenate, the *Roman Pontifical* perhaps is most noteworthy for what it does not include. There is no rite for becoming a catechumen and no scrutinies. It signals no liturgical or catechetical preparation for baptism throughout the season of Lent.

The sole exception is the delineation of the preparatory rites on Holy Saturday morning. These rites are referenced parenthetically in the texts for the Easter Vigil (32:1–39). The new fire was to be kindled at eleven in the morning or at noon. The pontifical interrupts its description of the service after the readings to explain that those to be baptized should have been "catechized" by means of the exorcism at nine in the morning. The ritual generally repeats the one from the tenth century, with these variations: It omits the inscription of the names and the directions for speaking half the ephphetha into each ear; in addition, the priest is to recite not just the Creed but also the Lord's Prayer during the final imposition of hands (13–18).

Then the pope baptizes the infant under a triple immersion, invoking the holy Trinity only once in this way: "I baptize you in the name of the Father." He immerses once. "And of the Son." He immerses a second time. "And of the Holy Spirit." He immerses a third time. "That you may have eternal life. Amen." *Roman Pontifical* 32:25

BAPTISM

The baptisms took place during the Easter Vigil. The bishop processed to the font and blessed the water (19–23). He prepared to baptize one, two or three infants, and the presbyter or deacon baptized the rest.

Each infant was received from a godparent, who was asked the child's name. The bishop continued, "N., do you believe in God the Father almighty, creator of heaven and earth?" "I believe," came the response, presumably from the godparent.

He asked about belief in Jesus Christ and in the Holy Spirit, and then inquired, "Do you wish to be baptized?" "I do," came the response, again probably from the godparent. The bishop then baptized the infant three times while reciting the formula (24–25).

Several rituals followed baptism. The child was returned to the godparent and was offered to the priest or bishop, who anointed the crown of the head with chrism while saying, "Peace be with you." Then came two rituals that had appeared in a different form or location in the tenth-century pontifical: A white garment was placed on the child, who also received a lighted candle (26–28).

The priest gives the newly baptized a candle, saying, "Receive this excellent candle. Take care of your baptism, so that when the Lord comes to the wedding banquet, you may go out to him in the heavenly hall." *Roman Pontifical* 32:28

The children were then confirmed if a bishop was present. The ritual took place as in the *Roman-Germanic Pontifical*. Here, though, the bishop imposed hands on the head of each of those to be confirmed before praying for the sevenfold gift of the Spirit. The formula also changed to, "N., I sign you with the sign of the cross, and I confirm you with the chrism of salvation, in the name of the Father and of the Son and of the Holy Spirit" (31–33).

All were given communion "according to the custom of individual churches," including the infants, even if no bishop was present to confirm them first. Infants who could not yet eat solid food received under the form of wine; the minister dipped a leaf or his finger into the blood of Christ for the child to suck (29).

LIFE AFTER INITIATION

The newly baptized attended daily Mass throughout the Easter octave to receive communion (37).

◆◆◆

The *Roman Pontifical* of the twelfth century eliminated the preparatory rites which seemed superfluous for a bishop's administration of infant baptism.

Preparation for Baptism

- The only prebaptismal rites took place on Holy Saturday morning, including exorcisms, the ephphetha, and the recitation of the Lord's Prayer and the Creed.

Baptism

- Baptism occurred during the Easter Vigil by a triple immersion, following a water blessing, profession of faith and a statement of intent.

- The crown of the child's head was anointed with chrism.

- A white garment and a candle were presented to the newly baptized.

- Confirmation with handlaying followed if the bishop was present.

• All the newly baptized received communion, whether or not a bishop was there to confirm first.

Life after Initiation

• The newly baptized returned for Mass and communion every day of the Easter octave.

The Pontifical of the Roman Curia
Handbook and Help

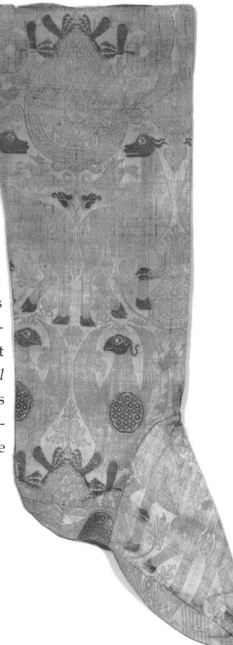

22

U nder Pope Innocent III (1198– 1216), the Roman Curia served the church as a traveling administrative body. Because of their many journeys, the members needed portable liturgical books. Innocent authorized a revision of the *Roman Pontifical* to suit their situation, but the results won wider popularity. Other itinerant preachers found the book helpful, and it gained more use than originally intended. When Pope Clement V (1305– 1314) moved the papal residence to his homeland in France to begin the seventy-year period when popes dwelled at Avignon, he brought along the *Pontifical of the Roman Curia*. It shows how rituals like those of the catechumenate developed according to the needs of the church in the early thirteenth century.

Musée Cluny: © R.M.N.

Pontifical stocking belonging to Cardinal Arnaud de Via (+ c. 1330).

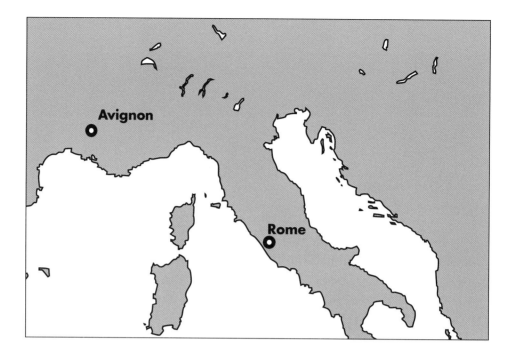

The *Pontifical of the Roman Curia* revised both the baptismal liturgy and its preparations (44, 53). This book restored the *Gelasian's* order for becoming a catechumen, which the twelfth-century *Roman Pontifical* had discarded, and enriched it markedly (53). Apparently conceived for adults who would speak during the rite, it included extra directions applying to infants.

PREPARATION FOR BAPTISM

The ritual proceeded in this way: The priest stood at the threshold of the church and questioned those becoming catechumens. "N., what are you asking God's church?" he inquired. "Faith," each would reply. "What does faith offer you?" he continued. "Eternal life." Then the priest gave a catechetical summary of the importance of the commandments and the concept of the Trinity. He exorcised the candidates, blowing into each one's face. He traced the cross on their foreheads with his thumb, saying "N., I place the sign of the savior, Jesus Christ our Lord, on your forehead." He did the same over each one's heart. Exhortation and prayers followed. The priest then placed his hand upon each one's head and prayed again. He exorcised salt and placed some in the mouth "of the infant," saying, "N., receive the salt of wisdom. May it be a benefit for you toward eternal life. Amen. Peace be with you." "And also with you." Exorcisms patterned on those from the *Gelasian* followed.

Then the priest brought the catechumens into the church, saying, "Enter into the holy church of God, that you may receive a heavenly blessing from our Lord Jesus Christ." Then the parent or godparent placed the infants on the ground and recited the Lord's Prayer and the Creed over them before picking them up. Placing infants on the ground may have imitated the ancient posture for scrutinies; lifting them up may have imitated the presentation of the infant Jesus in the Temple (Luke 2:28).

Even though it restored and elaborated the order for becoming a catechumen, the *Pontifical of the Roman Curia* followed the *Roman Pontifical* of the twelfth century by omitting the scrutinies.

BAPTISM

The order of service for Holy Saturday morning, mentioned parenthetically in the twelfth-century pontifical, does not appear in the thirteenth-century book. Some manuscripts of the *Pontifical of the Roman Curia* include it, but not on Saturday morning. It appears only during the Easter Vigil, an option permitted in the *Roman-Germanic Pontifical* of the tenth century.

The vigil began at noon with the blessing of the fire. While the scriptures were being read, one of the priests "catechized" the infants presented to him in a separate place for that purpose, by performing the rituals formerly associated with Saturday morning: He signed the forehead of the infants three times with his thumb while saying, "In the name of the Father and of the Son and of the Holy Spirit." He placed a hand upon their heads and recited the exorcism. He touched their nostrils and ears with his saliva and recited the ephpheta text. He led the renunciation of Satan. He anointed them on the breast and between the shoulders with the "holy oil" of catechumens. Then he imposed his hand on their heads again while he recited the Lord's Prayer and Creed (44:10–14). All then processed to the font for the blessing.

The baptism resembles that in the previous pontificals. The bishop asked the names of the children and if they believed in the Trinity. He baptized three of them with a triple immersion in the name of the Trinity. The junior deacons, cardinals and priest canons baptized the other children (44:20–22).

Several rituals followed. The priest anointed the crown of the head of the baptized. Then the children were clothed in white garments and each was given a candle. The bishop then confirmed the three he had baptized (44:23–26). Nothing is said of the confirmation of others; apparently since the bishop himself did not baptize them, they waited for another occasion to be confirmed. No instructions followed regarding communion at this Mass nor throughout the Easter octave. By this time, at the Fourth Lateran Council (1215) under Innocent III, the age at which one was obliged to receive communion once a year had been defined as the "years of discretion," and many discontinued the custom of infant communion almost immediately, even though the council had not forbidden it.

◆◆◆

The *Pontifical of the Roman Curia* adapted the baptismal rites by restoring an order for becoming a catechumen and reducing what followed baptism.

Preparation for Baptism

- Those seeking baptism took part in an expanded order of becoming a catechumen, including an opening dialogue at the door of the church, exsufflation, signation, prayer, handlaying, salt, entrance into the church and prostration.

- No scrutinies or other prebaptismal rituals appeared.

Baptism

- The rites formerly associated with Holy Saturday morning took place during the Easter Vigil: signation, exorcism, ephphetha, renunciation, anointing, handlaying and the recitation of the Lord's Prayer and Creed.

- Baptism followed in the customary way with the blessing of the font, the profession of faith and a triple immersion in the name of the Trinity.

- After baptism, the priest anointed the crown of the children's heads; they each then received a white garment.

- The bishop confirmed those whom he had baptized, but apparently not those who had been baptized by others.

- No rubric urged the newly baptized infants to share in the baptismal eucharist.

William Durand •23
Pontifical and Cornerstone

By the end of the thirteenth century the entire catechumenate required only a few hours. William
Durand recorded it in his pontifical (1292–1295),
the same book that introduced
a slap from the bishop in the
confirmation rite.

Upper half: Saint Paul curing the blind; lower half: Baptism
of Saint Denis, c. 1230–1250, Paris.

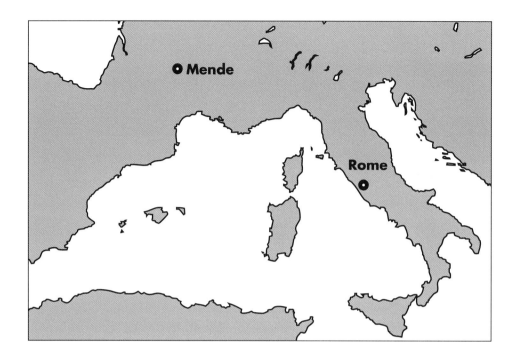

Durand, a French jurist, became bishop of Mende in 1286. He compiled a pontifical for use in his diocese, based on the three main earlier ones. Its organization and clarity eventually made it the foundation for subsequent editions of the *Roman Pontifical.*

Between the *Gelasian Sacramentary* and the *Pontifical of Durand,* the liturgies of the catechumenate underwent considerable modifications. Ultimately all liturgical preparation for baptism took place entirely within the context of the Easter Vigil.

"The infants to be baptized are catechized by some priest." That laconic rubric appears in the *Pontifical of Durand* after the scripture readings of the Easter Vigil (3:4, 12). It is the first mention of any prebaptismal formation or ritual in the book. Previously useful catechumenate rites were no longer practiced.

The order for making an unbaptized adult a catechumen, so expressive in the *Pontifical of the Roman Curia,* made no appearance in Durand's work. Nor did the scrutinies. Durand also omitted the Saturday morning rituals.

BAPTISM

The entire order of baptism, complete with the rites of preparation, took place during the Easter Vigil. The service began at noon with the blessing of the fire and its incense. After the scriptures, their psalms and their prayers, some priest "catechized" (exorcised) the infants to be baptized (12). Durand does not describe the ritual; the priest would have had to refer to another pontifical or ritual book to see how it was done.

The baptismal rite followed. The bishop processed to the font and blessed it elaborately. He asked the names of the infants and baptized them "in the customary way." Once again, Durand does not describe what that is; the bishop would have had to refer to a previous pontifical. He confirmed the infants on the forehead with chrism, using a new formula, "I sign you with the sign of the cross and I confirm you with the chrism of salvation. In the name of the Father and of the Son and of the Holy Spirit." He slapped them lightly on the cheek and said, "Peace be with you" (1:1, 3–4). Mass continued, and the bishop received communion (3:4, 14–19, 32). The newly baptized were given no instructions regarding communion at this Mass or during the week.

Although Durand only provides this one example of baptism, baptisms at Easter were rare by this time. Most children were baptized by priests in a single ritual shortly after birth.

◆◆◆

The developments in the catechumenate begun after the *Gelasian* continued in the work of Durand. The church compressed into one event all the rites which had not been suppressed.

Baptism

• Baptism took place at the Easter Vigil when the bishop presided.

  • After the scripture readings, priests exorcised those to be baptized.

  • The bishop baptized following one of the previous pontificals.

  • The bishop confirmed the newly baptized.

  • No evidence suggests that infants received communion at their baptism.

• Most infants were baptized by priests shortly after birth.

© 2000 Passionist Research Center.

Baptistry of the Church of St. Mary the Virgin, Great Bington, England, thirteenth century.

24 • Toribio Motolinía
Missionary and Historian

The twelve Spanish Franciscan friars who arrived to evangelize "New Spain" in 1524 astonished a group of natives, who regarded their unshod feet and threadbare habits, and repeated the word *motolinía*. Brother Toribio de Benavente asked what the word meant. "Poor," he learned. He adopted the description as his name.

Permission of Academy of American Franciscan History, Washington, D.C.

Toribio Motolinía. Detail from a painting in the Church of San Francisco, Puebla, Mexico.

From 1536 to 1541 Motolinía kept a diary of his ministry in Mexico City and its environs. Through it comes to light the way the first missionaries to the New World catechized and baptized the natives.

Toribio Motolinía reckoned that between 1521 and 1536, forty Franciscan missionaries had baptized more than four million natives in New Spain. Since there were other missionaries and other places being evangelized, he calculated the complete number of baptisms to be over nine million by the following year (*History* 2:2–3).

Some of the natives swam across the stream and asked the friars to come to its bank and speak the word of God to them. They went, and in the part where the river was narrowest they preached to them, the friars on one side and the Indians on the other. . . . They got the children to the other side on rafts, where the friars baptized them. *History* 2:2

The missionaries came from a church in which most of those baptized were infants, quite incapable of prebaptismal instruction. Nor did their ritual books carry rites for an adult catechumenate played out in stages; these had been long abandoned in Christianized Europe. Consequently the missionaries had little context or guidance for establishing expectations about prebaptismal instructions and ritual moments for adults completely unfamiliar with the Christian milieu.

FIRST INTEREST

According to Motolinía, friars began preaching in small towns where parents gladly permitted their children to be baptized after hearing the gospel (*History* 2:2). Adults and children then came in such great numbers that the missionaries had to baptize every day (*History* 2:3).

PREPARATION FOR BAPTISM

Although some accepted baptism after a single instruction (*History* 2:2), a lengthier preparation came into practice. The friars presented topics including the pope, scripture, the one God and creator, false idols, good and bad angels, the fall of Adam, the church, the justice of God, Moses and the love of God. These and the postbaptismal themes of Jesus and the sacraments were handed down in written sermons attributed to the twelve friars *(Sermons)*. Before the friars admitted any adult to baptism, they first examined his or her knowledge of Christianity, but the large numbers of converts rendered such individual attention difficult. Some natives became so nervous that they could not recite the Lord's Prayer, the Hail Mary and the basics of the faith, as requested. Motolinía was inclined to accept even these on good faith (*History* 2:4).

BAPTISM

Baptism in mission countries posed some problems. The friars did not have ready access to all the materials for baptism, and the numbers of those approaching them proved greater than what the Roman rite of baptism ever envisioned. The Franciscan, Augustinian and Dominican missionaries disagreed about the solutions and actually discontinued baptisms from time to time, to the loss of those who desired it (*History* 2:4).

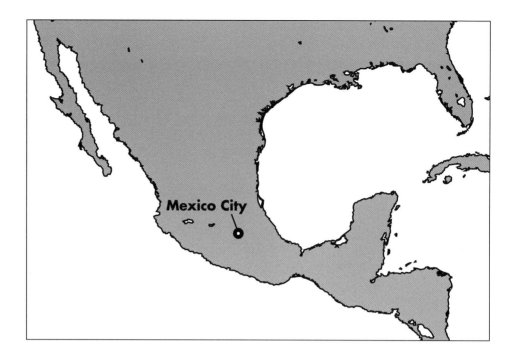

Motolinía describes an early attempt at adaptation. The missionaries faced two or three thousand baptisms a day, requiring the ephphetha and exsufflation, a burning candle in a windy courtyard, individual white garments and entrance into a church building in a place where there was no church building. They also had to learn the local language and teach catechism. Some other way of baptizing had to be devised. Motolinía says they first tried it this way: They gathered those to be baptized, placed the children in front and conducted the service over all of them.

Some priests who begin to teach the natives would like to see them as holy in the two days that they were working as they would have been after ten years of teaching. *History* 2:4

The friars performed the ceremonies of the cross, breath, salt, saliva and white garment over only a few, and then baptized all the children individually. They gave a final instruction to the adults, reminding them what to believe, what to reject, and how to live in marriage (monogamously, for example); then they baptized each adult individually (*History* 2:4).

Other missionaries disputed these adaptations, questioning their validity and even their morality. The Augustinians decided in 1534 to use the complete ritual and to baptize only on four days a year: Christmas, Easter, Pentecost and the feast of St. Augustine (Basalenque 1:2). To accomplish this required the services of two priests: All in the region came to the village chosen for the ceremony, where the church, houses and streets had been decorated with greenery for the occasion. Those to be baptized wore their cleanest clothes and formed a line. Each priest exorcised half the group, then one walked down the line anointing all the foreheads while the other administered baptisms at the font. They divided the other rites between them in a similar way (Ricard 92).

A group of missionaries and bishops could not resolve the matter at a meeting in 1536 and sent the question about adaptations to the archbishop of Seville, Spain, who deferred it to the pope and permitted them to continue whatever they were doing in the interim.

Pope Paul III responded with a bull in 1537, *Altitudo divini consilii.* He declared that the missionaries who had abbreviated the rites had not sinned, but that the full Roman rite should be followed except in urgent necessity. He required four things for baptism: blessed water; individual catechism and exorcism; the rites of salt, ephphetha and garments for only two or three of the entire group; and the use of oils for all—chrism on everyone's head and the oil of catechumens on the breast, except for women, who could be anointed on another part of the body for the sake of modesty.

The missionaries convened a synod of bishops and superiors in 1539 to discuss the implementation of Paul III's bull. They left the extent of catechesis to the judgment of the individual priests, but they remembered and recommended the forty-day preparation of Lent with its "fasts, exorcisms, catecheses and scrutinies" (Synod of 1539, 13). They abbreviated the exorcisms as much as possible. They accepted the pope's wish that everyone be anointed. They reserved adult baptisms to Easter and Pentecost and defined "urgent necessity" as siege, shipwreck, perilous sickness and national insecurity (Synod of 1539, 1–2); many, however, had argued unsuccessfully that the missionary world itself constituted "urgent necessity."

According to Motolinía, the Franciscans resolved not to baptize adults at all at this point because the approved rites for children and the sick were shorter. In time, though, they relinquished this strategy due to the overwhelming number of requests from adults. They baptized with full ceremony. Motolinía says in five days he and one other priest baptized over 14,200 natives, complete with the anointings with oil of catechumens and chrism (*History* 2:4).

The 1539 synod also called for the publication of a text the priests could use in administering the sacraments, a practical measure exercised in many regions. The *Manual for Adults* appeared in 1540, but no complete copy of it survives. A new ritual was published in 1560, but priests still used the 1540 text for baptisms until late in the century. According to the sixteenth-century *Franciscan Code,* the baptismal text in the 1540 manual was drawn from the thirteenth-century *Pontifical of the Roman Curia,* but it combined the order of becoming a catechumen with the order of baptism into one celebration, as the *Roman-Germanic Pontifical* had done.

Cliché Bibliothèque nationale de France, Paris.

Painting from a Mexican codex, c. 1572. Although much of the image is difficult to decipher, the lower right clearly shows the baptism of an Indian.

Concerns about adequate baptismal preparation for adults remained for some time. The 1552 Council of Lima required thirty days. The First Council of Mexico (1555) forbade the baptism of those who had not been properly catechized. "We have been informed that the adults who want to be converted to our holy faith, whether Indians in the country or Negroes of Guinea, have not been well instructed about that which they should believe before being baptized. Therefore we declare that no priest, religious or diocesan, has the right to baptize an adult who has not been sufficiently instructed in our holy and catholic faith, who is not validly married, and who has not completely renounced paganism and returned stolen goods" (*First Council of Mexico*, 1555).

Before Motolinía died in 1568 the Mexican bishops had published the *Manual of Sacraments* (1560), which included an order for baptism. It followed the custom-ary practice and placed all the rites in one ceremony: asking the name, exsufflation, signation, salt, exor-cisms, the Creed, the Lord's Prayer, the ephphetha, renunciation, confession of faith, expression of intent for baptism and the baptism itself—by pouring, not by immersion. Chrism on the crown of the head, the garment and the lighted candle followed.

When some were told they could not be baptized, they said, "In no way will we leave here without baptism, even if we know we have to die here."

History 2:4

The same manual required adults to have knowledge of four areas before baptism: the Lord's Prayer, the Creed, the commandments of God's law and of the church, and the sacraments. These four themes followed the traditional divisions of catechisms; they were soon organized in the *Catechism of the Council of Trent*, first published in 1566.

Although these missionaries and councils had recommended a time of prepa-ration, they did not precisely call it a catechumenate. The ecumenical Council of Trent (1545–1563) issued no canons on a catechumenate, nor were any missionary bishops in attendance.

◆◆◆

First Interest

- People expressed interest in Christianity based on the presence and preaching of missionaries.

Preparation for Baptism

- Catechesis preceded baptism, from as brief as a day or two to as long as several weeks.

- Those to be baptized were questioned concerning their knowledge of the Lord's Prayer, the Creed, and the basics of the Christian faith.

Baptism

- Baptism followed the Roman rite; the missionaries did not separate the catechumenal rituals.

- Some adaptations were made because of the numbers being baptized; for example, only a few in the group received all the ceremonies, or ministers shared responsibilities.

- Missionaries baptized adults almost every day, not just on Easter and Pentecost.

- Other adaptations deferred to local sensibilities; for example, missionaries avoided anointing women on the breast.

Life after Initiation

- After baptism the neophytes continued their education in the sacraments.

25 ◆ Alessandro Valignano
Visitor and Promoter

Everard Mercurian, General of the Society of Jesus, appointed the Italian-born Alessandro Valignano (1539–1606) Visitor to the East in 1573, days after Valignano had made his solemn profession following a relatively brief time with the Society. With that appointment, he accepted full responsibility for all the Jesuit missions and missionaries from Mozambique to Japan. In three visits to Japan (1579–1582, 1590–1592, 1598–1603), Valignano built upon the work Francis Xavier had begun from 1549 to 1551. He developed a plan of evangelization, formed natives for ordination to the priesthood, popularized Christianity in Japan, and promoted the cultural adaptation of the Roman church to the needs of the Far East.

Image courtesy Edizioni di storia letteratura.

Alessandro Valignano.

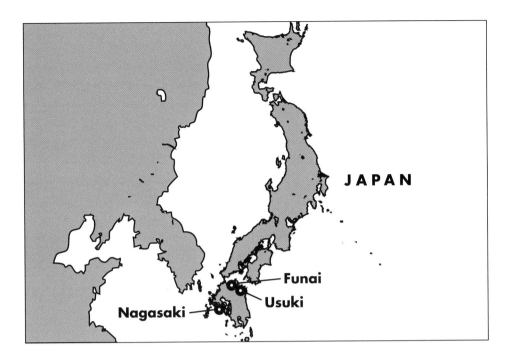

During his time of leadership, missionaries discovered the need to provide cate-chetical background for the natives who hungered for baptism. They found useful a catechetical structure that the liturgical books had abandoned: the catechumenate.

The mid-sixteenth-century missionaries to Japan met a people who accepted baptism in great numbers. The Japanese favored Christianity for many reasons. One, as Valignano noted, was a God-given curiosity to hear and embrace the presentations of the missionaries. They found in Christianity the road to salva-tion; the reasonableness of its teaching appealed to their intellects and invited their conviction. Other, lesser motives probably also played a role, including increased possibilities for trade, associ-ation with foreign powers, the coercion of the missionaries and of the rulers of their own countries. When one leader wished to gain power against a non-Christian opponent, he could promote Christianity in order to win allies. Valignano admitted that many became converts because of the will of their superiors.

The Japanese are inspired to become Christians of their own free will, convinced by reason and with the desire for their salvation. . . . The Japanese receive our doctrine much better than other people and make themselves proficient with it and the sacraments in a brief time. After they have converted they let go of everything, their idolatries, that which in all the other people of the Orient is backwards. Valignano, *The Importance of This Enterprise*

Missionaries reported groups of converts in the dozens, hundreds and thou-sands. The authentication of conversion needed close attention. Pedro Gómez, Vice Provincial of the Jesuits, wrote in 1594, "It is not permissible to force pagans of this kind to receive faith and baptism" *(Compendium of Catholic Truth)*.

Missionaries labored to provide solid catechetical formation to those seeking baptism. Their converts would have accepted baptism almost immediately, but a group of consultors meeting with Valignano in 1580–1581 argued that a slower preparation promised greater merit. A more deliberate preparation would increase their work, but they believed it would yield greater rewards. "It is better that the provinces be made Christian than remain pagan. . . . Among pagans they are surrounded by many dangers. . . . Relief and remedy for our work will follow. . . . Being fearful is to distrust divine Providence. . . . In our experience as Christianity increases so does the stronger reception of religion."

Valignano affirmed the efforts to improve catechesis. In 1582 he reported to his superior, "Many are baptized with the proper disposition, and before they may be baptized they are catechized in the best way possible." He recommended having a separate room for catechesis, someplace "recollected and remote" (*Ceremonial* 1:39). It would prove useful in following their plans to allow preparation for baptism to take some time.

The idea of restoring something like the catechumenate was already being advanced elsewhere in the East. In 1567 the First Council of Goa (in India) had recommended three months of preparation for baptism (2:37). Many missionaries were offering less, some as little as two or three days of catechesis. The council's recommendation influenced a change in many places, but the results were neither immediate nor universal. The Third Council of Goa in 1585 ordered, perhaps begrudgingly, that no baptisms take place without twenty days of catechesis (26).

The Sacred Synod orders that . . . baptism should not be given until three months after requesting it, because experience has shown that some of those regress after being baptized. First Council of Goa (1567) 2:37

With too few priests to conduct all the required instructions, the missionaries trained catechists to assist them. With few printed books they relied on catechumens to write down the teachings and prayers. Some catechists offered instructions in the morning and evening for adults, and at noon for children. "Three or four times almost every day now we have preaching here for the catechumens," reported Luis Frois from Usuki, Japan, in 1577. These instructions taught hearers about belief in God and challenged them to reject Japanese sects. Catechumens heard an exposition of Christian doctrine, including a presentation of the Ten Commandments. Many adults were baptized after a few weeks of these sessions, but the missionaries questioned each one about Christian doctrine beforehand.

A sample of the topics for instruction is found in J.L. Gay's reconstruction of the 1600 *Catechism of Nagasaki:*

1. God the creator of all things.
2. The mystery of the most holy Trinity.
3. The Incarnation: Jesus true God and human, born of the Virgin Mary.
4. The eternal destiny of our soul.
5. Jesus has taught us the road of salvation, giving us the commandments, the sacraments (baptism is especially treated), and his church.
6. The passion of Christ: its redemptive work by means of the cross.
7. The resurrection of Christ; its significance: he has received all power.
8. The final work of Jesus: he will raise up all and will be judge of the living and the dead.
9. The meaning of baptism and confession: This is to pardon sins committed against the commandments.

10. The eucharist: the meaning of the priest, the Mass, and the presence of Jesus.

11. God is everywhere. The importance of prayer; one must recite the prayers the church has taught us.

BAPTISM

Valignano asked that baptism be administered with all reverence, following "the necessary order" (*Ceremonial*, Appendix 1:185). Missionaries were expected to follow the current Roman ritual, baptizing on Easter, Pentecost or another Sunday. Large groups at a time approached the sacrament. The number of Christians in Japan rose from 150,000 in 1582 (about 1 percent of the total population) to 240,000 in 1590 *(Jesuit Archives)*.

The Japanese subject to their superiors are easily converted when their superiors command them and they understand that it is their will. And this is the door through which those who are baptized usually enter at the beginning, and in this way we begin to be received in Japan and to make Christians in different places. Valignano, *East Indian Summary*

At least one missionary began the rite with the inscription of the names of those to be baptized. Luis de Almeida's letter of 17 November 1563 explains how he baptized a group of 170 people who had attended his lectures for ten to twenty days. The catechumens approached the altar, on which was "a beautiful image of Our Lady of Grace. Then were inscribed the names of all those who it appeared to me were prepared to receive the sacrament of baptism, and thus together with the pagan name the Christian name was inscribed for them." He did this to imitate the church fathers, "who, holding the names of each one on a sheet of paper, put it in their hand when they were about to baptize so that they could know the names." He explained the ceremonies to the catechumens and then baptized them.

Some accommodations had to be made, even though the missionaries desired to follow the Roman rubrics. The rare appearance of bishops hampered efforts to obtain consecrated oils every year, so the missionaries in the East received permission from the popes to omit those ceremonies, and to replenish the oils every three or four years (*Jesuit Archives* 40). The anointings posed an additional problem: The Japanese deemed it immodest for men and women to remove part of their clothing for the priest to administer the anointing. Papal permission to omit the anointing acquiesced to that point also. "Since there has been no bishop up to now in Japan it was not possible to obtain holy oils for baptism. . . . It seems appropriate to us by virtue of our privilege not to anoint the baptized, partly because we have no oil, and partly because it appears a very indecent thing to make noble men and women remove clothing from the breast and shoulders" (Organtino Gnecci-Soldi, *Jesuit Archives* 12, II, f. 242).

In 1598 Luis Cerqueira, recently appointed bishop of Japan, consulted with a group of missionaries and accepted some pastoral solutions to problems in the administration of baptism stemming from the Japanese concern for cleanliness and the consequent resistance among the natives to having someone touch them. Since a resident bishop could consecrate oils in abundance, the ceremonies formerly omitted for lack of oil could be restored. But the personal concerns of the Japanese prevailed over this measure and occasioned several adaptations. As a result, when reciting the ephphetha, the priests would omit placing saliva on the nostrils "because this is very strange among the Japanese." Instead, with their thumb they traced a cross on the nostrils and ears of children to be baptized, and over the nostrils and ears of adults without touching them. Instead of tracing the sign of the cross upon the bare breast and head of catechumens, the priests made them over their clothing. Instead of placing salt directly into the mouth of catechumens, they handed a spoon of salt to the adults who tasted it themselves; they gave spoons to the godmothers to place salt in the mouths of young children, although the priests were also permitted to do this themselves. The size of the crowds led to an additional accommodation here: If the number to be baptized was large, catechists and religious brothers were permitted to assist with the salt.

Although the Roman rite at the time permitted baptism by immersion, pouring or sprinkling, missionaries sensitive to the Japanese were advised to baptize only by pouring water over the catechumens and into basins. Oils were administered with the feather of a bird. The bishop thought it prudent to introduce the traditional Roman ceremonies to the Japanese slowly, a strategy he advised was more important "than the small diversity which one will be able to notice in doing some ceremonies for adults and children" (*Consultation* of 1598).

The baptismal font could be a more elaborate apparatus. A description of the font at the church of Funai written in 1581 explains the usage of a local fountain which integrated elements of Japanese life into baptism. The turtles of the fountain's sculpture symbolized eternal life; the pine tree signified happiness. "For the font on Holy Saturday we had to do nothing because the king had ordered it done in the Japanese manner. There was in the fountain an orange tree which had leaves of silk and many oranges of gold, and a pine tree which had needles of green raw silk, hard enough to appear prickly if put in one's hand. On each branch there was a magnificent pine cone, like those around here, very natural. There was also some bamboo of which the trunk was wooden, and the silk leaves, so natural, that one could barely tell they were artificial. In the middle of the fountain there was a very beautiful and natural turtle, which appeared, at least when the water came to its feet, that it wanted to jump in" (Luis Frois II, p. 309). After baptism the missionaries completed instructions on the other sacraments, including a series on confession and communion (Frois, p. 162).

The freedom with which Valignano and his missionaries worked was short-lived, not because of papal concerns but due to local politics. By the seventeenth century the persecution of Christians in Japan had begun in earnest, and Japan closed its doors to missionaries—and to the West—for 250 years.

◆◆◆

First Interest

- People expressed interest in Christianity out of curiosity, a desire for salvation, intellectual conviction or forceful influence.

Preparation for Baptism

- Missionaries gave a series of instructions to catechumens, probably lasting a few weeks.

Baptism

- Baptism was administered following the Roman ritual with all the rites in one ceremony.

- Cultural adaptations were made to avoid touching those to be baptized.

Life after Initiation

- More instruction followed baptism.

26 ◆ Giulio Santori
Editor and Revisionist

The catechumenate almost reappeared in Roman liturgical books in the late sixteenth century — nearly 400 years before it finally did. The Council of Trent (1545–1563) had called for the promulgation of several new books. Its catechism was issued almost immediately, in 1566, a sign of the importance of education to the church. The breviary was revised in 1568, and the missal followed in 1570. But the *Roman Ritual,* the collection of the other rites including baptism, took longer to publish. In 1575 Pope Gregory XIII chose Cardinal Giulio Antonio Santori (1532–1602) to edit the new *Roman Ritual.* Santori envisioned a restoration of the catechumenate period, complete with time for catechetical preparation and a series of liturgical rites. He worked on the project for nearly thirty years.

Art Resource.

The Council of Trent attributed to Titian (c. 1488–1576). Louvre, Paris.

There were many reasons for reintroducing the catechumenate. Theologically, the restoration of the catechumenate honored the integrity of baptism; catechetically, it responded to the Council of Trent's call for religious education; pastorally, it fulfilled the needs of missionaries; and liturgically, it promoted a uniformity in books and customs among parishes and dioceses. Santori's principal interest, however, was probably the preservation of historical texts. In this and other sections of his work he decided to restore some of the ancient prayers of the church, lest they be lost. Still, he boldly proposed to restore the prebaptismal period and the rites that the liturgical books had omitted for hundreds of years.

Santori's work drew inspiration from the *Liber sacerdotalis* of 1523, the "priest's book" which contained basic rituals for ordinary use. He also benefited from the research of Melchior Hittorp, who published a collection of ancient rituals in 1568. There Santori would have seen the rich development of the prebaptismal rites which the church had more recently abandoned.

Santori had prepared an entire series of orders pertaining to baptism, including the baptism of children, scrutinies and solemn Easter baptism, processions during Easter week, the removal of the white garments, scrutinies and solemn baptism for Pentecost, and a celebration for the anniversary of baptism. He also composed essays explaining the meaning of the catechumenate and of mystagogy, the first systematic treatment of these periods. Where the more recent rituals spoke only of the "infants" to be baptized, Santori restored the word *catechumens.*

Santori died in 1602, when his work had reached its final stages. He had already requested the decree of publication from Pope Clement VIII. Unfortunately, the discussions surrounding his work were still incomplete when Clement also died. His successor, Paul V (1605–1621), created a new commission to edit the *Roman Ritual.* They completed the work in two years, publishing it in 1614, more than fifty years after the close of the ecumenical council. The new commission withdrew the catechumenate from the final draft of the *Roman Ritual.* In its place the commission created a single, extensive ritual of adult baptism, formed from many catechumenate rites. Some missionaries obtained and used many of Santori's suggestions about a catechumenate, largely through the efforts of the Carmelite Thomas de Jésus (1564–1627), who discovered Santori's work in the cardinal's library in Rome and appended it to a publication of his own which recommended prebaptismal catechesis in the missions.

CATECHESIS

When unbaptized adults sought life in Christ, Santori envisioned that they would go through a formal rite of admission to the catechumenate. A bishop or his delegate would examine their motives by testing their sincerity, investigating their choice of livelihood, and consulting their acquaintances. The church's minister was to invite them to renounce their first religion. They were to give their names to a notary and declare their desire to become Christians and to follow the commands of the church. They would also promise to present for baptism their young children who did not yet have the use of reason. Candidates' spouses and their mature children below the age of 25 would have to agree to participate in catechetical preparation, even if they later refused baptism. After declaring these intentions to

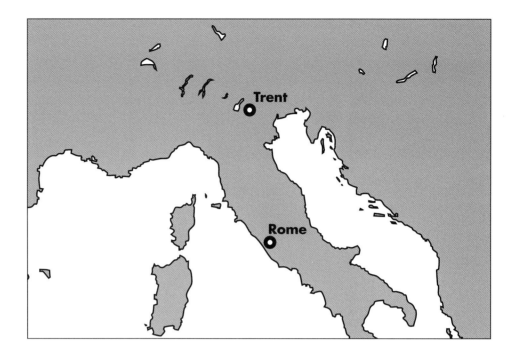

the notary, those desiring baptismal formation would remove any clothing that differentiated them from Christians. Their names would then be inscribed among those preparing for baptism. The minister would pray and give thanks, offer them Christian clothing, invite them to renounce Satan and confess faith in the Trinity, blow into their faces, sign them with the cross, and impose hands. Then they were to enter a "house of catechumens."

Catechumen houses had already been established in Rome and in several other cities as places where Jews and Muslims interested in Christianity could come for formation. Ignatius of Loyola conceived the idea in Rome, setting up two houses, one for men and one for women, in 1543. These were not just schools, but actual residences for catechumens, hosted by a priest catechist. (Houses for neophytes were established in 1562 and 1577 for those who had been baptized and wanted to further their formation or prepare to evangelize others of their people.) Catechumens gathered for morning and evening prayer, exorcisms, blessings, instruction and labor for the sake of the community. Santori wanted to use these houses of catechumens and improve their work with a more formal arrangement of ritual welcome and restored scrutinies. He recommended a formation of 40 days—more or less, depending on individual needs—which need not have coincided with Lent.

When any adult, enlightened by divine grace, decides to come from paganism to faith in our Lord Jesus Christ, he or she should be encouraged to go swiftly to the church. Santori, *Ritual* 125

Catechesis would cover the usual areas: the Trinity; the prophets, apostles and evangelists; creation and Adam's sin; good and evil; judgment and eternal life. Catechumens would learn the Sign of the Cross, the Creed and the Lord's Prayer, and they would tour the appointments of nearby churches. Santori did not recommend a specific catechetical text, but relied upon the skills of the catechist.

The cardinal gave few details about the scrutinies he proposed. He saw them more as an examination of the catechumen's faith rather than an exorcism in the ancient sense. In fact, they primarily introduced the rite of baptism. Santori said nothing about the presentation or recitation of the Creed and the Lord's Prayer.

BAPTISM

Santori recommended that the catechumens come to the font having fasted for two or three days, that they be vigilant in prayer and possess purity of heart. They were to bring white garments, supplying also those needed by the poor. In addition, Santori envisioned a solemn baptism on Easter and Pentecost, although the celebration was allowed at other times. His order for baptizing at the Easter Vigil (Santori, *Ritual* 55–76) called for the blessing of the font, baptism by immersion, confirmation by the bishop and communion of the adult neophytes and of children having the use of reason.

The scrutiny is an examination of the faith and the Christian religion, made by the priests and clerics upon those who demonstrate the desire to come to it, in order that they may be formed by its doctrine and by ecclesiastical discipline, so that, diligently examined and superbly instructed, progressing from day to day, they may be made worthy to receive the grace of baptism. Santori, *Ritual* 21

For hundreds of years the liturgical books had alluded to the confirmation of the newly baptized and omitted their reception of communion. Santori planned to give them more prominence.

LIFE AFTER INITIATION

The neophytes were to remain in the catechumen houses for forty days after baptism, when they would hear further instruction about baptism, the other sacraments, and on living a moral life. They were to strengthen their spiritual life in prayer, receive communion daily and remove their white garments on the Sunday after Easter. The leaders of the catechumen houses were to keep in contact with them for a year.

◆◆◆

Giulio Antonio Santori envisioned the restoration of the catechumenate as part of the *Roman Ritual* to be promulgated after the Council of Trent. This restoration never came to pass.

Catechesis

• Cardinal Santori recommended the restoration of the rite of entrance into the catechumenate, including an investigation of motives, renunciation of past belief, declaration of intent, change of clothing, inscription, prayer, exsufflation, signation and handlaying.

Preparation for Baptism

• Catechumen houses were established in many cities to provide a residence especially for Jews and Muslims who wished to join the church.

- They were to spend about 40 days in preparation, learning the basics of Christianity.

- Santori recommended a restoration of scrutinies, as an examination of the catechumen's knowledge.

Baptism

- Baptisms were conducted in the traditional way on almost any Sunday; Santori wished to restore immersions, confirmations at Easter and communion for the newly baptized.

Life after Initiation

- Some neophytes remained in houses to continue their formation.

The Roman Ritual 27
Convention and Standard

In 1614 the *Roman Ritual* revised after the Council of Trent was published. It complemented the 1570 *Roman Missal.* The *Missal* contained the prayers and other texts for Mass throughout the year; the *Ritual* provided the texts for other services. With very little alteration, the order of adult baptism from the *Roman Ritual* remained the standard throughout the Catholic world for almost 350 years; the *Missal* for almost 400 years.

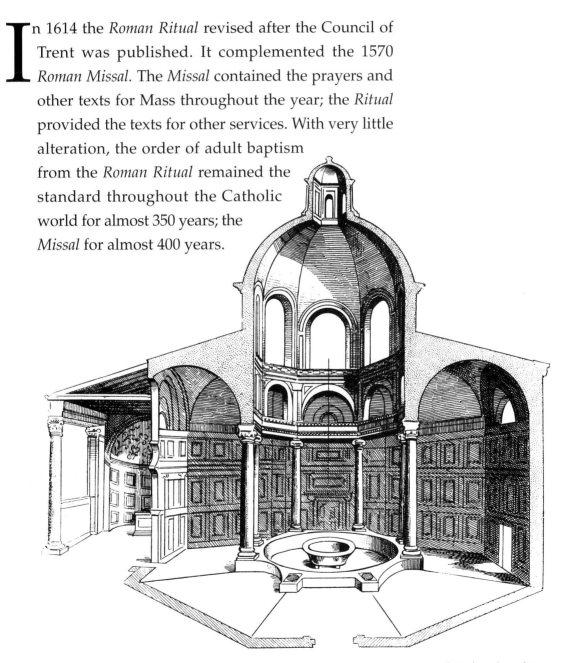

Lafreri's engraving of the baptistry at the Lateran basilica in Rome, 1540. H. Leclercq, "Baptistère," in *Dictionnaire d'archeologie chrétienne et de Liturgie,* vol. 2, Paris: Letouzey et Ané, 1907.

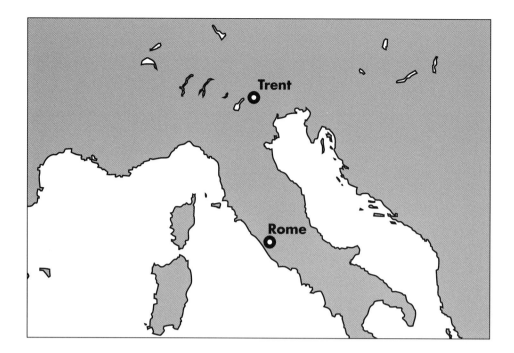

The 1570 *Roman Missal* included very little about the catechumenate. Although previous sacramentaries and pontificals contained a selection of prebaptismal rites, this one promulgated no such texts. During Lent, for example, where the scrutinies had appeared in liturgies of the past, they are absent from the 1570 *Missal*. The gospels of the woman at the well, the man born blind, and the raising of Lazarus still were proclaimed at Mass on Friday of the Fourth Week of Lent and Wednesday and Friday of the Fifth Week of Lent respectively, but no scrutinies accompanied them throughout the life of the *Missal*.

At the Easter Vigil, the *Missal* made provisions for baptisms. The Vigil was to begin after the office of Nones; ideally Nones would begin at three in the afternoon, but in reality they could have started at any time during the day. In fact, parishes generally began the Easter Vigil in the morning of Holy Saturday. After the blessing and lighting of the fire and the readings from the prophets, but before the Gloria, the *Missal* described an extensive blessing of the font. There followed this rubric: "If people needing to be baptized are present, the priest baptizes them in the usual way." In 1570 that "usual way" relied on previously published rituals, such as the *Roman Pontifical*, the *Pontifical of the Roman Curia*, the *Pontifical of Durand* or some version of those at use in the local church.

Adults should not be baptized unless they know it and want it and have been thoroughly instructed. Above all adults should be admonished to feel sorrow for their sins. *Roman Ritual 2:3*

In the 1614 *Roman Ritual,* however, the new "usual way" of baptizing was published after a serious revision of what Cardinal Santori had advocated. The *Ritual* contained no catechumenate period, and it situated the traditional rites in the place to which they had migrated, at the beginning of the order of baptism. It made no special effort to encourage baptisms at the Easter Vigil; in practice most were conducted on other occasions.

CATECHESIS

The *Ritual* expected that adults would be instructed and would express their desire for baptism, but it offered no further explanation. In parishes, the local priest usually conducted this preparation himself, meeting with the candidate in private.

BAPTISM

The *Ritual* created two separate rites, one for children and one for adults. The rite for children was shorter, and it preserved the more dominant role for the godparents of children who could not speak.

The adult rite made extensive use of catechumenal texts. It began with psalms and prayers, then it borrowed from material in the *Pontifical of the Roman Curia.* The priest went to the church doors where he met the "catechumens" (a term the *Ritual* used to identify the unbaptized adults), the men on his right, the women on his left. He asked their names and what they sought, then gave a catechetical summary on eternal life.

Next came a preliminary exorcism. It began with the renunciation and profession of faith. The priest then performed both an exsufflation and an insufflation: He breathed on the "catechumens'" faces and pronounced the exorcism, then inhaled in front of their faces in the form of a cross and invoked the Holy Spirit. He traced the sign of the cross with his thumb on their forehead and breast and asked them to renounce their former beliefs. With more prayers he then signed each of the "elect" (the term used by the *Ritual* here) with his thumb on their forehead, ears, eyes, nostrils, mouth, breast and shoulders, and then over their whole body. Part of this rite had appeared in the *Gothic Missal.* More prayers followed, the last one calling for handlaying on the heads of the "elect." The priest blessed salt, put it into the mouth of the "catechumens" and recited the appropriate prayers.

The next exorcisms were inspired by the existence of three scrutinies in the early Roman rituals. The priest invited the men among the "elect" to kneel and recite the Lord's Prayer. They then rose, and the priest signed them on the forehead and pronounced an exorcism while imposing his hand. This same ritual unit (kneeling, Lord's Prayer, standing, signation, exorcism and handlaying) was repeated two more times. Then the priest conducted the same threefold exorcism for the women. Thus the *Ritual* preserved the old Roman tradition of three exorcisms, but offered them back to back, first for men, then for women.

The priest then led the "elect" into the church, placing his left hand on their right arm or inviting them to hold the end of his stole. Inside, they prostrated themselves on the ground in adoration. Similar actions had appeared in the *Pontifical of the Roman Curia.* When they arose, the priest imposed a hand on their heads, and the "elect" recited the Creed and the Lord's Prayer. The priest imposed his hand again and offered another exorcism. He then performed the ephphetha, touching their ears and nostrils with his saliva. They renounced Satan again, and the priest anointed them on the breast and between the shoulders with the oil of catechumens.

Then they went to the font. If the water had not been blessed, the priest blessed it. He asked, "Do you believe?" in the Father, Son and Spirit. They responded, "I believe," each time. He asked, "What are you asking for?" "Baptism," they replied. "Do you want to be baptized," he pressed. "I do." Godparents placed a hand on the elect, who loosened the clothing around their necks and bowed over the font. The priest poured water over their heads in the form of a cross three times while saying, "N., I baptize you in the name of the Father *(pouring the first time)*, and of the Son *(pouring the second time)*, and of the Holy Spirit *(pouring the third time)*." He baptized men before women. A displaced rubric sanctioned baptism by immersion where it was customary, but by noting this permission at the conclusion of the entire rite, the *Roman Ritual* avoided encouraging this practice.

The usual postbaptismal ceremonies followed. The priest anointed the crown of the head with chrism, dried his thumb with cotton and offered the newly baptized a white garment and a candle. They were then dismissed. If a bishop was present, he confirmed them. If it was convenient, Mass followed and the neophytes received communion.

The *Ritual* made an accommodation to the missions of the Indies and the New World still struggling with large numbers of converts. It permitted them to perform all the rituals on only a few catechumens or to omit some of the ceremonies altogether. Due to the complexity of this rite, many pastors needing to baptize adults actually used the simpler rite for children.

◆◆◆

Catechesis

- Some unspecified formation should have preceded the baptism of an adult. In parishes the priest himself usually conducted this in private.

Baptism

- The Easter Vigil permitted baptisms, but most were conducted on other occasions.

- The rite of baptism began with psalms and prayers, then assumed many of the rituals of the former catechumenate, including an opening dialogue, a catechetical summary, renunciation and profession, exsufflation, exorcism, insufflation, signation, repudiation of heresy, more signations, prayers, hand-laying, salt, three exorcisms inspired by the scrutinies, entrance into the church, prostration, the recitation of the Creed and the Lord's Prayer, the ephphetha, renunciation of Satan and anointing, the blessing of water, profession of faith and statement of intent.

- Baptism was administered most commonly by pouring in the name of the Trinity.

- The anointing with chrism and the white garment immediately followed baptism, but generally not confirmation or the eucharist.

Louis-Simon Faurie •28
Innovator and Loyalist

Bishop Étienne-Raymond Albrand (1805–1853), the vicar apostolic of the province of Kuei-chou in China, designated Louis-Simon Faurie to succeed him. When Albrand died, Faurie objected to the appointment, because at the age of 29 he had been ordained a priest for only two years. Pope Pius IX finally persuaded him to accept seven years later.

© Corbis.

Ruins of the Church of Saint Paul in Macao, China, built in 1602 by Japanese refugees and burned down in 1853.

In the face of persecutions, massacres, civil war, famine and pestilence, Faurie led a prosperous mission far from his home in Bordeaux. He attended the First Vatican Council in Rome in 1870, but he fell ill and died after his return to Kuei-chou in 1871. During his ministry he worked hard with his priests for the conversion of the natives, who approached baptism through a three-stage catechumenate.

The three-stage catechumenate had been developing for quite some time among the Chinese missions. As early as 1665 the Sacred Congregation for the Propagation of the Faith was encouraging missionaries to spend at least 40 days preparing adults for baptism. The Congregation, founded in 1622 under Pope Gregory XV, attempted to correct the lack of unity among the church's missionaries throughout the world.

In 1722 the Vincentian Johann Müllener, the vicar apostolic of Szechwan, had asked the Propagation of the Faith about the restoration of a four-stage catechumenate in China. His mission was already developing a catechumenate of one to two years. The Congregation responded in 1724 with an indirect reply: "His Holiness has decreed that, when the necessary points have been considered regarding a sufficient instruction of catechumens for the necessary and appropriate time according to the quality and capacity of the individuals, all the ceremonies and exorcisms according to the order prescribed in the *Roman Ritual* should be observed." So the Parisian missionaries in China assumed it was all right to organize a catechumenate in stages and to divide the adult rite of baptism into the appropriate parts. In 1801, the Congregation left the length and content of the catechumenate up to the judgment of the vicar apostolic.

Indeed, some catechetical and liturgical needs persisted. Faced with large numbers of catechumens, missionaries had already tried omitting some of the ceremonies in the baptismal rites. However, Pope Benedict XIV rescinded the permission to shorten the rites in 1744: "In baptizing children or adults of whatever sex or condition we strictly prohibit that the sacramentals be omitted; rather, all should be practiced openly: the signation with saliva, salt and the insufflation."

The missionaries in Tonkin tried another solution: baptizing people of all ages according to the more simplified children's order. This practice offered more uniformity in the administration of baptism and aided their attempts to baptize large numbers of converts. But in 1797 the Congregation replied, "What is prescribed in the *Roman Ritual* must be completely

Art Resource.

Façade of Palazzo di Propaganda Fide (Propagation of the Faith) by Gian Lorenzo Bernini, seventeenth century, Rome.

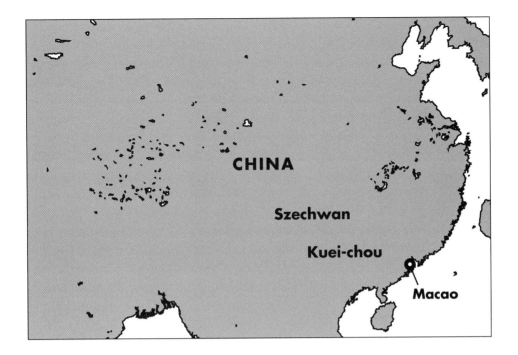

observed except in case of necessity." In 1803 the Congregation relented and permitted the use of the children's order in case of genuine necessity, lack of time or the fatigue of the missionaries. But in 1851 the Congregation reverted to its former position: "The *Roman Ritual* should stand."

In this environment, Bishop Faurie was working with the presumed permission for a catechumenate of some length and the division of the order of baptism into two parts. Even before he arrived in Kuei-chou, the catechumenate had three identifiable stages: adoration, the catechumenate and baptism.

In 1848, a few years before Faurie was even ordained, a report from Kuei-chou described the adoration. Natives received teaching about religion, and when they decided to become Christian they signed themselves with the cross. They were then brought to an oratory or to an altar in the home of a Catholic family. Two candles were lit on the altar, and an experienced Christian knelt with each pagan, who held a paper with the necessary prayers in hand.

The ceremony began with the Sign of the Cross. The pagans then prostrated themselves five times, confessing their faith in God and Mary, and renouncing their past errors and sins. They recited the Creed, the Lord's Prayer, the Hail Mary, the Ten Commandments, the Two Great Commandments, five prayers of thanksgiving and the Sign of the Cross. Christians from the community welcomed and congratulated them, and they became known as *adorers.*

In 1865, Bishop Faurie made a report to Rome about life in the missions; it included his report on baptism. He admitted one problem with confirmation: Priests were confirming infants at baptism. Some priests had received this permission from Rome when they worked in faraway places, but they were supposed to wait until the children were about the age of seven to confirm. Now many priests were confirming children who had access to the bishop, and the children were receiving the sacrament too young. Faurie proposed that he permit only the oldest priest in each zone to confirm, in hopes that the custom would die away.

But more significant was his report about baptismal preparation. He explained the three-stage catechumenate that had been in place before his arrival, and he proclaimed his support for it. He found it useful for testing the faith of catechumens and he hoped the practice could continue. Faurie wrote, "The infidel who converts to the faith approaches the regenerative bath by a triple degree: adoration, the catechumenate and baptism.

"(1.) Adoration: Infidels who believe after hearing talk about religion are brought to the oratory. Two lighted candles are placed on the altar, or in individual homes before the crucifix or some religious image. The printed paper is put into their hands so that they may recite the prayers of adoration.

"(2.) Catechumenate: When the adorers know and believe the principal dogmas of the faith, mainly the Holy Trinity, the incarnation, redemption and baptism, they are admitted to the catechumenate. To confer the catechumenate we perform on them the ceremonies of baptism of adults up to the ephpheta inclusively. Then we permit them to pray in the church with the Christians, to assist at the holy sacrifice. They are not separated from the baptized because of a lack of availability of places where the holy mysteries are usually celebrated.

"(3.) Baptism: When the catechumens know the sum of all Christian doctrine and observe faithfully the rules of the religion, they are admitted to baptism. Then we finish the ceremonies of baptism of adults, by beginning at the place after the ephpheta where one says again, 'What is your name?'

"The rite of adoration does not seem to me to be an abuse, for it is not practiced as an ecclesiastical rite and it is not forbidden in any way to belong to the sacrament of baptism. It is a simple manifestation of one's adherence to faith."

But the abuse may be in the separation of the catechumenate and baptism, for the *Ritual* does not indicate explicitly that the ceremonies of baptism of adults should or may be performed on many occasions separately. Apparently the church has not addressed this question.

"I discovered this usage in place in this way, and I watch it accordingly until it may be otherwise directed by the church. I can affirm one thing: this gradation of adoration, catechumenate, and baptism is very useful to test the faith and the behaviors of the proselytes, and I would like, if the holy canons do not oppose it, that it be kept in the future" (*Report to Rome*, 1865).

He got his reply in 1866. The Congregation responded that there was no problem with a catechumenate of one or more stages; however, dividing the order of baptism in the *Roman Ritual* "cannot be approved in any fashion. This usage is contrary to the practice of the Roman church."

In 1867 a disappointed but obedient Faurie sent an instruction to his priests, inviting them to maintain the practice of the adoration for the pagans, but "when they will be able to be admitted to baptism, all the ceremonies of baptism will be performed on them as they are found in the *Roman Ritual*." In remote places he permitted baptisms whenever the priest arrived, but wherever a priest resided, he reserved baptisms to the vigils of Easter and Pentecost, and to the Saturday before Christmas.

The Sacred Congregation for the Propagation of the Faith, supported by a similar report the same year (1866) from the Sacred Congregation of the Holy Office, suppressed the missionaries' liturgies of the catechumenate.

◆◆◆

First Interest

- Pagans heard missionaries' general instructions about Christianity.

- They underwent a ceremony of "adoration," professing faith in God, renouncing their former way of life, and reciting the Creed, Lord's Prayer and other Christian texts.

- They were welcomed by the Christian community and were called "adorers."

Catechesis

- Adorers continued their formation for some length of time.

- They began the "catechumenate" stage with the first part of the order of baptism from the *Roman Ritual,* up to the ephphetha.

Baptism

- When catechumens had proven themselves ready, they were baptized with the remainder of the order.

29 ◆ Charles Lavigerie
Founder and Model

It was only fitting that a teacher of history would firmly replant the catechumenate on the continent where the term originated, Africa. Charles Martial Allemand Lavigerie (1825–1892) served as a churchman in his native France and taught ecclesiastical history at the Sorbonne. Named bishop of Nancy, he harbored a love for the missions of the church. In 1867 he became bishop of Algiers, and the following year was named apostolic delegate of West Sahara and Sudan. Also in 1868 he laid the foundations for the Society of Missionaries of Africa, called the "White Fathers" because of their white habits. He founded the Missionary Sisters of Our Lady of Africa in 1869. Together these groups carried out his vision of evangelizing the African continent. He was named a cardinal in 1882 and two years later became the archbishop of Carthage, the home of Tertullian, and primate of Africa. He died in Algiers in 1892. During his lifetime the manuscripts for the *Apostolic Tradition* (1848), the *Didache* (1873) and Egeria's diary (1884) were discovered.

Courtesy Missionaries of Our Lady of Africa, Algeria.

Charles Lavigerie.

When Lavigerie sent his missionaries to equatorial Africa in 1878, he structured a catechumenate for them to follow, informed by early practice and based on directives from the Congregation for the Propagation of the Faith. By observing the order of baptism in the *Roman Ritual,* Lavigerie secured the approval of Pope Leo XIII. Within fifty years missionaries in virtually every corner of Africa were preparing adults and children for baptism by means of the catechumenate.

Missionaries had already been evangelizing Africa for a hundred years or so when the Congregation for the Propagation of the Faith sent Italian Capuchins to the Congo in 1645. They worked under extraordinarily difficult conditions, amid poverty and disease, with few missionaries, numerous converts and a poorly structured method of instruction. Already in 1650 they sought advice from the Congregation about baptizing without much catechesis, a practice based not on their many responsibilities, but on their dim view of the natives: "Is it possible to baptize adults who have a very hampered intelligence and are deprived of all culture, and who therefore can neither understand nor learn the truths of the faith, and who dwell far from a priest, simply 'in the faith of the church' like infants, if they say they want to believe all that which the church believes?" The Congregation responded with like disparagement, "If their free assent is clear, they may be baptized, even if they lack the culture and are not capable of learning what they are taught. For as infants and the uncommunicative who do not have the use of reason are baptized 'in the faith of the church,' one may baptize those who are born with a culturally natural incapacity."

[Requirements for passage to the catechumen stage include the following:] (1.) Having completed the period of testing prescribed for postulants, (2.) having responded in a satisfying manner to an investigation of their religious knowledge demanded by the mission, (3.) and being found in the conditions of life which are not an obstacle for future baptism.

Bishops of the Belgian Congo, 1926

As the centuries progressed, missionaries gained more success catechizing the African church. When Lavigerie's missionaries set about their work with a specific plan, the benefits appeared immediately.

Lavigerie's catechumenate had three groups: postulants, catechumens and faithful. Postulants demonstrated a serious desire for the Christian life, catechumens made intense preparation for baptism, and the faithful were taught the meaning of the sacraments after baptism. He envisioned that each of the first two stages would require two years of preparation. The time could be shortened for those most outstanding in their formation and for children of catechumens.

CATECHESIS

The purpose of the first period was to free the postulants from their adherence to paganism and to win their belief in God. The natives faced the formidable obstacles of fetishism and polygamy, which were deeply entrenched in their culture. Catechists offered sessions up to two or three times a week at the missionary centers; postulants spent up to two years at this stage. The topics they heard were based on instructions from the Congregation for the Propagation of the Faith: the existence of God, the immortality of the soul, the Ten Commandments and the

hope of salvation. They also learned basic Christian prayers, the Lord's Prayer and the Creed. By mixing intellectual and moral formation, catechists hoped to obtain a firm commitment to the Christian faith and a readiness to abandon pagan ways. Postulants finally showed their intent by destroying any pagan idols at home and dismissing all wives but one.

They will establish among their neophytes three distinct orders. The first will be the order of "postulants," to which will be taught only the fundamental truths of the natural order, clarified by revelation: the existence of God, the immortality of the soul, the distinction between good and evil, the moral law as the Ten Commandments teach, suffering and recompense in the afterlife. . . . The second will be that of "catechumens," to which will be revealed the essential truths of Christianity, but without speaking to them about worship and the sacraments other than baptism. Finally the third will be that of the "faithful" for whom there will no longer be secrets.

Lavigerie, "Instructions to Missionaries"

PREPARATION FOR BAPTISM

To pass to the second period required an examination of knowledge and conduct. The ceremony of passage included a public renouncing of pagan ways and a profession of Catholic faith. Promising to remain a faithful follower of Christ forever, the postulants formally asked for baptism. They received a distinctive sign—a cross or a medal—which they wore upon their breast. With this ceremony they became catechumens and progressed to the next stage.

During the catechumenate the preparation continued with both intellectual and moral formation. The topics expanded to include what was necessary for baptism. Lavigerie warned catechists about being too rational or philosophical about the Christian faith. They frequently taught by concrete examples and parables.

Before baptism another examination took place. Catechumens needed evidence of their participation in sessions, their behavior, their capability for perseverance, their marital status and their knowledge of Christianity.

BAPTISM

When the missionaries judged them ready for baptism, their names were published and they made a retreat three days before the event. They were baptized in the morning of a feast day before a large number of the faithful. Mass and communion followed.

LIFE AFTER INITIATION

Courtesy Missionaries of Africa, Washington, D.C.

Infant baptism in Africa.

After their baptism, the neophytes learned about the other sacraments. They remained in their groups for a while to help make the transition into Christian life. They learned about the frequency of confession and communion, and about common Catholic religious practices.

During the next fifty years this plan was discovered, adapted and put into place by missionaries throughout Africa. The time of preparation, its content and the ritual passage between stages all varied somewhat.

The White Fathers in the Sudan followed Lavigerie's program. The Holy Spirit missionaries developed a catechumenate only gradually, but they lengthened it within a short period of time.

In French West Africa, a one-year catechumenate was required in Dahomey (Benin) in 1899. French Guinea started at eighteen months in 1907 but expanded to two years in 1921. Nigeria required one year in 1898, eighteen months in 1912, and three years in 1918. In Togo, missionaries expected one year for those living on the coast, but two and a half years for those in the rural inland. In 1921 the Ivory Coast lengthened its preparation from one year to two and a half.

The story repeated itself in French Equatorial Africa. Missionaries in Cameroon, Ubangui-Shari (Central African Republic), Gabon and Angola expanded catechumenates from two to three years between 1906 and 1915. Many of them divided the time evenly into two stages of preparation.

It is necessary in order to have solid conversions that they take place in a group, so that the neophytes may be supported by one another.

Lavigerie, Letter to Livinhac, 1881

A series of episcopal conferences in the Belgian Congo in the first half of the twentieth century called for a two-year prebaptismal catechumenate, and some bishops added another year. The White Fathers in the same area stayed with their four-year approach there and in Rwanda.

To the south, South Africa and Madagascar called for a two-year catechumenate. In British East Africa around the lakes of Nyassa, Tanganyika and Victoria, the White Fathers and the Holy Spirit Fathers followed the four-year schedule of preparation. In 1912 the bishops of East Africa established one year of postulancy and two years of the catechumenate. Bagamoyo required four years, the Upper Nile two to three years, and Dar Es Salaam three to four years.

In short, Lavigerie's White Fathers (as well as the Holy Spirit missionaries) brought a developed idea of the catechumenate to Africa. Baptismal preparation became longer, more organized and universally accepted. Support for this evolution derived not just from theory or history, but from the actual lived experience of missionaries.

◆◆◆

First Interest

• People were inspired by the preaching of missionaries.

Catechesis

• Initial catechesis of postulants included fundamental truths about God, the rejection of pagan practices including polygamy, and basic Christian formation.

• Postulants met with catechists two or three times a week for up to two years.

• Those seeking to become Christians underwent an examination of their understanding and behavior.

• They rejected paganism, and the men dismissed all wives but one.

• Postulants became catechumens in a ritual. They renounced pagan ways, confessed the Christian faith and received a cross or a medal.

Preparation for Baptism

• Preparation for baptism required more sessions with catechists about deeper Christian truths. It lasted up to another two years.

• Missionaries also observed the catechumens' moral conduct.

• Catechumens passed another examination about their behavior and understanding.

• When they were accepted for baptism, their names were published and they made a three-day retreat.

Baptism

- Baptism took place in a group before a large gathering in the morning of a feast day.

- Mass and communion followed.

Life after Initiation

- Neophytes continued their formation in the Catholic way of life and its sacraments.

30 ◆ Joseph Blomjous
Petitioner and Partitioner

Born in the Netherlands, Joseph Blomjous (1908–1990) eventually became bishop of Mwanga in Tanganyika (since 1964, part of Tanzania). Impressed with the effectiveness of the catechumenate stages in Africa, he sensed that these periods could be enhanced with liturgical rites if the order of baptism for adults in the *Roman Ritual* could be partitioned for separate occasions.

Photo courtesy of the Archdiocese of Mwanza, Tanzania.

Joseph Blomjous.

In 1959 he became the first bishop to submit to the Apostolic See an acceptable plan for the restoration of catechumenate rites. The Sacred Congregation of Rites finally agreed and published its first catechumenate in April of 1962, six months before the opening of the Second Vatican Council. The climate for the restoration of the catechumenate was growing, not just in the missions but also in Europe.

Paulette Gouzi of the Mission of Paris experimented with a catechumenate in dechristianized areas of the city in 1945. She and her colleagues discovered young Parisians who had never been baptized. They offered them a fruitful preparation by forming a group of catechumens. Prior to this time, the success of the catechumenate had been noted in mission countries; it had not occurred to church leaders to develop it among disenfranchised youth in countries such as France.

Gouzi advised preparation in a community that embraced education, spiritual growth and moral development, accompanied by ceremonies that suited the needs of the unbaptized. She preferred that baptism take place in a large group at the Easter Vigil, and recommended the use of the vernacular language in addition to Latin.

The number of adult candidates for baptism continued to grow after World War II, as candidates moved by spiritual conversion, social relationships or nuptial plans presented themselves. Over the next several years French bishops appealed to pastors for a prebaptismal preparation of at least three months, including participation in parish life and prayer. But they still envisioned that candidates for baptism would be prepared individually.

In 1951 Pope Pius XII authorized the restoration of the Easter Vigil to the evening as a worldwide liturgical experiment. The response was so favorable that he approved the new Easter Vigil for the entire church in 1953. In 1955 the Sacred Congregation of Rites introduced additional reforms for the rest of Holy Week. It also gave permission, after centuries of requests, to divide the order of baptism for adults into two parts. The first part could be celebrated in the morning on Holy Saturday.

The Jesuit missionary J. Christaens published an article in 1956 praising the benefits of the catechumenate in Africa, but calling for the retrieval of its rites. "Would there not be a place in our contemporary catechumenates—I think above all in our African missions—to reestablish the liturgical rites which would mark out as in former ages the long road of adults toward baptism?" Xavier Seumois, secretary general of the White Fathers, expressed similar sentiments at a congress in Montserrat in 1958.

But it was Bishop Joseph Blomjous of Tanganyika in 1959 who sent to the Holy See the request for the restoration of the catechumenate, together with a recommendation for its structure. He envisioned seven steps drawn from the *Roman Ritual:* inscription, three scrutinies, the combined ceremonies of presenting the Creed and the Lord's Prayer, exorcisms on Holy Saturday morning and baptism at the Easter Vigil. This petition came at a time when Rome was hearing voices for the restoration of the catechumenate not just from the missions, but also from Europe.

At the Vatican the request went to the Congregation of Rites with the support of Cardinal Ferdinando Antonelli, who had helped orchestrate the reform of Holy Week. The restructuring of adult baptism joined the list of tasks in the growing

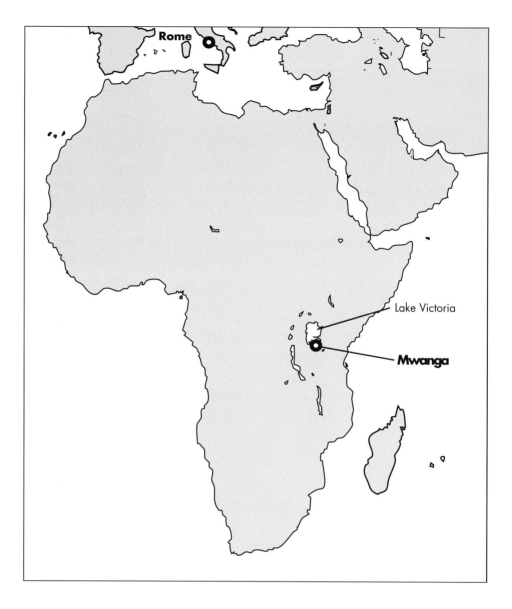

liturgical renewal. The Congregation of Rites needed doctrinal approval from the Holy Office; it consulted the Propaganda of the Faith because of the implications of the revised rite for missionaries; it also needed authorization from the recently elected pope, John XXIII. In spite of the possible hindrances, the Sacred Congregation of Rites published the "Order of Baptism of Adults Arranged as a Catechumenate in Steps" in April of 1962, an extraordinary year that also saw the publication of revisions of the *Roman Pontifical* and the *Roman Missal*—all before the opening of the Second Vatican Council that fall.

The 1962 Order was published as an alternative to the one-step baptismal rite; it did not completely replace the traditional order of adult baptism in the *Roman Ritual.* The new Order

Christianity is not an individual religion and from the beginning future Christians should learn to put their soul in common with others. . . . This preparation will not be only doctrinal. . . . It is necessary that they learn to pray and love God. . . . They must also learn to live among Christians. Paulette Gouzi, "Adult Catechumenate in a Dechristianized Milieu"

appeared in seven steps, but slightly different from those envisioned by Bishop Blomjous. The congregation divided the bishop's first step in two and combined his fifth and sixth steps. Each began with an opening versicle, "God, come to my assistance."

PREPARATION FOR BAPTISM

The first step followed the *Roman Ritual's* order for baptizing adults up to the blessing of salt. It no longer suggested meeting at the door of the church (a rubric moved to the sixth step), no longer separated men from women and no longer called for the repudiation of heresy. It permitted godparents to

If persons to be baptized are present, especially if they are many, it is permitted to anticipate that morning at a convenient time the ceremonies of the *Roman Ritual* which precede the actual conferral of baptism, that is, in the baptism of infants up to the words "Do you believe in God?" and in the baptism of adults up to the words "What is your name?" Sacred Congregation of Rites "Instruction on Holy Week" 14

administer the signations, or the catechumens could sign themselves while the priest made a cross over the group. This first step included the following: All recited psalms and prayers. The priest called the names of the catechumens. He asked them, "What do you ask from God's church?" "Faith," they replied. "What does faith offer you?" "Eternal life." Then the priest gave the catechetical summary. He invited them to renounce Satan and to profess their faith in the Trinity. He blew onto their faces in exorcism and inhaled over their faces in prayer for the Holy Spirit. (Where breathing seemed inappropriate he could extend his right hand while reciting these texts.) He traced the sign of the cross on their forehead and breast. (The rubrics alternate calling the group "catechumens" and "elect.") More prayers followed, and then the signations on the forehead, ears, eyes, nostrils, mouth, breast and shoulders of the catechumens. A prayer and dismissal concluded the first step.

The second step emphasized the giving of salt to signify "the growing sweetness of the catechumens in Christian instruction." The priest blessed salt, offered a prayer and then placed salt in the mouths of the catechumens, or, if the bishop permitted, had the catechumens place it into their own mouths. They were then dismissed.

As the third, fourth and fifth steps, three exorcisms were designated, but the ritual permitted local bishops to decide if the three should be separate or combined into one ceremony. Bishops could also require only one scrutiny and omit the other two. During the exorcism, the priest invited the men to pray, kneel and recite the Lord's Prayer. They rose. He invited godparents to sign them together with him. He prayed to God and then exorcised the devil. The priest then followed the same procedure with the women. They were all then dismissed. The fourth and fifth steps repeated the structure of the third.

At the beginning of the sixth step, the priest met the catechumens at the door of the church or outside. He invited them into the church, where they prostrated themselves on the floor. The priest invited them to arise, and, extending his hands over the "elect," he prayed the Creed and the Lord's Prayer with them. He invoked another exorcism, then conducted the ephphetha, using his saliva to touch the ears and nostrils of the catechumens. (For a reasonable cause he could omit the use of

L'Osservatore Romano Photo Service.

The opening session of the Second Vatican Council at St. Peter's Basilica, Rome, October 1962.

his saliva and the actual touching of the catechumens.) Then he asked each by name to renounce Satan. He anointed them with the oil of catechumens on the breast and between the shoulders; this could be omitted if it caused difficulties, and replaced with another signation and exorcism. The priest dried his thumb on cotton and then prayed another exorcism to conclude the ceremony. All were dismissed.

BAPTISM

The final step took place at the baptismal font. Those to be baptized were called *elect.* The priest called them by name and asked them to confess their belief in the Trinity and to state whether they wished to be baptized. With godparents assisting, baptism took place as the ritual had described it for hundreds of years: The elect bowed over the font; godparents placed a hand on them; the priest poured water three times while saying the baptismal formula. For the first time in any Roman order of baptism, the 1962 ritual omitted any mention of immersion. The priest anointed the newly baptized with chrism on the crown of the head; this could also be replaced with a sign of the cross if the anointing caused difficulties. Their godparents gave the "elect" a white garment and a burning candle while the priest recited the appropriate texts. The "neophytes" continued holding the burning candle if confirmation followed. All were dismissed. The ritual did not specify a time of year, but it was cast in a way that invited the celebrations to culminate on Easter.

Although this alternate way of initiating adults was published in 1962, it was still relatively inaccessible. In 1965, following Vatican II, the theologians working on the new order of initiation referred to the *Roman Ritual* instead of the 1962 texts because the latter were "difficult to find and the formulas are almost always the same."

◆◆◆◆

Catechesis

- Some instruction should have preceded baptism at least for a few months.

- The instruction was generally carried out in private.

Preparation for Baptism

- The order of baptism from the *Roman Ritual* was split into seven parts. The first six, including all the prebaptismal rites, could be celebrated before baptism.

- Step one followed the *Roman Ritual* up to the signations.

- Step two was the giving of salt.

- Steps three, four and five were exorcisms. These could be combined or reduced.

- Step six featured the recitation of the Creed and the Lord's Prayer, the ephphetha, renunciation and anointing.

- Adaptations were permitted for places where some of the ceremonies (for example, the use of saliva, touching the catechumens or anointing them) would present difficulties.

Baptism

- Baptism and the postbaptismal rites took place according to the *Roman Ritual.*

- Immersion was not presented as an option.

31 ◆ Balthasar Fischer
Educator and Chair

The full catechumenate was reborn under the patient and learned direction of Balthasar Fischer. After the close of the Second Vatican Council, the implementation of the Council's wishes fell to many study groups. To revise the initiation rites, the fathers turned to Fischer, a former student of liturgical theologian Joseph Jungmann, and a professor at the seminary in Trier. Fischer (1912–) was ordained to the diocesan priesthood for Trier, the birthplace of Ambrose, in 1936, and began his career as a professor in 1945. In 1961 he served on the preparatory commission for the Council, and after the Council he chaired the twelve-member Study Group 22, which revised the catechumenate.

Harry Breen, © 2000 Passionist Research Center.

Baptistry, Holy Cross Church, Champaign, Illinois.

In addition to Fischer, Group 22 included the following members: Frederick McManus, a diocesan priest from Boston and canonist at the Catholic University in Washington (United States); Aemilius Lengeling, a diocesan priest from Münster and professor at the university there (Germany); Ignatius Oñatibia, a diocesan priest from Vitoria and professor at the seminary there (Spain); Boniface Luykx, OPRAEM, a specialist in the African experiences (Belgium); Aloysius Stenzel, SJ, a specialist in infant baptism and former professor at the Jesuit Faculty of Frankfurt (Germany); Aloysius Ligier, SJ, a professor at the Gregorian University in Rome (France); Joseph Lecuyer, CSSP, another professor in Rome (France); Jean Baptiste Molin, FMC, a specialist in the prayers of the faithful (France); Jacques Cellier, a diocesan priest and founder of the first modern catechumenate in Europe (France); and Corbinian Ritzer, OSB, a monk of the Abbey of Schäftlarn and a specialist in the rites of matrimony (Germany). Xavier Seumois, one of the White Fathers promoting the catechumenate in Africa, served as secretary (Belgium). Together this group developed the revised order for the Christian initiation of adults from 1965 to 1969, in a series of reports and drafts. After the first round of meetings, Cellier, who would later become the national director of the catechumenate in France, succeeded Fischer as the chair.

At the beginning, however, Fischer helped educate people. Drawing on his study of the catechumenate's history, his knowledge of the *Roman Ritual*, his conviction of the relevance of the *Apostolic Tradition*, his sensitivity to tradition and his commitment to pastoral advantage, Fischer taught the Council fathers how the catechumenate had blossomed in the early church before undergoing the simplification of its structure. Aware of the missionary success with a catechumenate in stages and of the growing interest in modern Europe, he persuasively crafted a series of changes in the order for adult initiation that built on the insights of the optional 1962 Order and dramatically altered the baptism of adults in the *Roman Ritual* for the first time since its publication in 1614.

The study group completed a provisional text by 1966 and received approval from Rome to experiment with its application. Fifty pastoral centers in Japan, Indonesia, Mali, Togo, the Ivory Coast, Upper Volta, Rwanda, Zaire, Congo, Belgium, France, Canada and the United States received the new text and tested it until 1969. The study group reviewed the reports from these centers before finishing its work that year with a revised order. That order went to the Congregations for the Doctrine of the Faith, for Sacraments and for the Propagation of the Faith. Final approval waited for the revised order of confirmation, which was being handled by another study group. The Congregations authorized a few revisions before the order of adult initiation went to Pope Paul VI for his approval, which he gave in 1972. After that, the ritual was translated and adapted by episcopal conferences around the world with approval from the Vatican. The 1974 provisional English translation of the *Rite of Christian Initiation of Adults* in the United States was replaced by the standard translation in 1988. This publication followed the work of a subcommittee appointed by the National Conference of Catholic Bishops: Bishop Joseph A. Ferrario (chair), John Cummins, Robert Duggan, James Dunning, Luanne Durst, Raymond Kemp, Ronald Krisman, Ronald Lewinski, Don Nuemann, James Notebaart, Barbara O'Dea and Karen Hinman Powell.

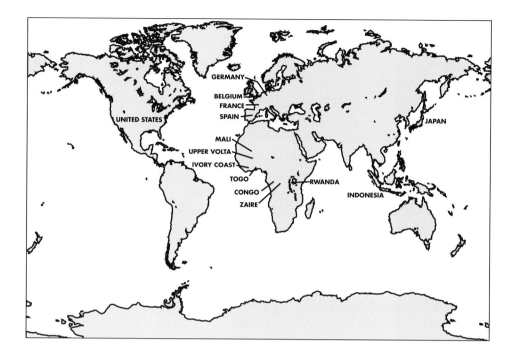

Throughout the period of its development (1965–1969), the new order received accolades and criticisms from those who experimented with it. Pastoral centers the world over praised its general structure, its division of preparation into two periods of formation, its relevance to contemporary needs, the improvement of its prayers, adaptations, options, new creations and the acknowledged role of catechists. However, they voiced many concerns they hoped would be clarified before its publication: the remoteness of the antiquated terminology, the need for promoting and not just permitting local adaptation, too little ritual involvement for catechists, the complicated steps, the appearance of a precatechumenate when some communities had none, the negative implications of its concept of conversion, the intricacy of the rite of acceptance, the inappropriateness of dismissals, the absence of rites in the catechumenate period, the artificiality of the rite of election and the presentations, the number and language of the scrutinies and their repetitious prayers, imprecision about the minister and occasion of confirmation, the empty state of mystagogy and the contradiction of saying the community should be involved when the rites gave them so little to do. The study group went to work on simplification and adaptation, but they hoped that experience with the rituals and familiarity with the introductions to them (which had not yet been written) would clarify many of these matters.

Though published as liturgy, the concept of the catechumenate relied on catechesis. The document was born out of a liturgical need: Missionaries had already built a catechetical structure and they needed rituals to support it. However, once those rituals were in place, they sparked a revolution in catechesis and in the faith communities that gave birth to new members. Christiane Brusselmans (1930–1991) in Belgium, James B. Dunning (1937–1995) in the United States and others in pastoral work promoted the catechumenate as a means for entire parishes to celebrate, catechize, form community and serve. They captured the spirit of the study group's intent, involving the entire community in baptismal preparation, not just the parish priest. As Balthasar Fischer liked to say, "Not the shepherds make sheep. Sheep make sheep."

Overall, Vatican II's order of adult initiation stresses the role of the community, a catechesis embracing both intellectual and moral formation, and the personal connection between ministers and catechumens. The study group operated from the assumption that the order of infant baptism should be derived from the one for adults, not vice versa. It accepted its mandate from the Council's *Constitution on the Sacred Liturgy* (CSL), *Sacrosanctum concilium*, which called for the revision of both the 1614 order of adult baptism and the 1962 version in stages, for the restoration of the catechumenate (CSL 66), for the easy comprehension of sacramental signs (59), the intimate connection of confirmation with the whole of Christian initiation (71), and the importance of baptismal and penitential themes of Lent (109). The finished order of initiation presented the revised rite in stages, but also preserved a one-step version for pastoral necessity, an abbreviated rite for emergency use over which a lay person could preside, notes on the rituals for baptized but uncatechized adults and something completely novel—a catechumenate designed for children. Easter was the expected time for adult baptism, according to a tradition dating to Tertullian; however, exceptions were permitted.

The revised catechumenate envisions four periods separated by three liturgical steps. The precatechumenate brings basic spiritual formation to those inquiring about faith. The first step accepts them into the order of catechumens. The second period is the "catechumenate" properly called, during which extensive formation takes place. The second step is the Rite of Election, beginning the third period, purification and enlightenment, which usually coincides with Lent. The third step, the rites of initiation themselves, takes place at the Easter Vigil. The fourth and final period is mystagogy, a catechesis for those enlightened by baptism.

The rite of Christian initiation presented here is designed for adults who, after hearing the mystery of Christ proclaimed, consciously and freely seek the living God and enter the way of faith and conversion as the Holy Spirit opens their hearts. *Rite of Christian Initiation of Adults* 1

FIRST INTEREST

The first period, evangelization, applies to those expressing some first interest in Jesus Christ. They hear the mystery of Christ as the Holy Spirit opens their hearts (*Rite of Christian Initiation of Adults* 1; all references are to the U.S. edition). Spiritual experience, preaching, community—whatever first stirred their interest—finds occasion to flower. Some of those experimenting with the rites in the late 1960s recommended that they open with some ritual for "sympathizers" to mark the beginning of evangelization. The study group did not endorse this recommendation, but permitted conferences of bishops to provide "a preliminary manner of receiving those interested . . . without any ritual celebration" (39).

CATECHUMENATE

The first step, "Acceptance into the Order of Catechumens" in English (41), carries a title in Latin that literally means, "order for making catechumens," drawn from

© 2000 Passionist Research Center.

Baptistry, Cathedral of the Assumption, Louisville, Kentucky.

the *Gelasian Sacramentary.* The study group honored requests that the rite should celebrate a human welcome into the community and appear less as an exorcistic repudiation of a former way of life. Admitting that this step does not carry the importance of baptism at Easter, the members made little effort to invite the entire community; the introduction suggests that if not everyone, then at least friends, acquaintances, catechists and priests should be there (45, 48). It neither recommends nor dissuades a Sunday celebration.

The new version opens with "Receiving the Candidates": greeting, opening dialogue, candidates' first acceptance of the gospel, affirmation by the sponsors and the assembly, signing of the candidates with the cross and invitation to the celebration of the word of God. The liturgy of the word follows with its instruction, readings, homily, optional presentation of a Bible, intercessions for the catechumens, prayer over the catechumens and dismissal of the catechumens. It includes optional rites of exorcism, renunciation of false worship, giving of a new name and presentation of a cross.

The informal greeting may include some explanation of the ceremony (49); the study group recognized that it would be unfamiliar to many who participated. This replaced the opening psalms and prayers of the *Roman Ritual,* which the study group omitted to avoid prolonging the ceremony.

The dialogue that follows the greeting (50–51) comes from the *Roman Ritual,* which itself drew from the *Pontifical of the Roman Curia.* It begins outside the church, as the *Pontifical* had suggested (48). The study group found that this dialogue corresponded to the investigation of motives and sincerity of conversion required in the *Apostolic Tradition.* But the question, "What do you ask of God's church?" even resembles the question Peter asked at the threshold of the house of Cornelius, "Why have you sent for me?"

The candidates' first acceptance of the gospel (52) begins with the catechetical summary also in evidence from the *Pontifical of the Roman Curia.* It acknowledges the evangelization that led the candidates to conversion. The study group amplified this summary with references to John 17:3 and Philippians 2:5. It also offered optional texts for the first time, as well as permission for the celebrant to adapt the summary to the candidates' answers in the preceding dialogue. This summary concludes when the celebrant asks the candidates if they accept this gospel.

The study group removed the renunciation and profession of faith that formerly occurred here, since it seemed to duplicate a ritual more appropriate at baptism. The candidates' first acceptance of the gospel (52) more appropriately replaces the profession of faith.

The exorcism and renunciation of false worship formerly in the rite at this point have become optional at the discretion of episcopal conferences (70–72). The exsufflation, exorcism and renunciation of false worship may replace the candidates' first acceptance of the gospel. The study group feared that candidates would not understand these rituals or that the exorcism would incorrectly imply personal demonic possession. The insufflation, added to the 1614 ritual, was omitted because it seemed premature for the disposition of the candidates, anticipatory to the work of baptism and inappropriate for catechumens, while it diminished the exorcism.

The affirmations by the sponsor and the assembly (53) give opportunity for an initial witness to the candidate's disposition, a value that had already surfaced in the story of Cornelius.

The signations begin with the signing of the candidate's forehead with the cross (54–55). The meaning of this gesture is clarified in the prayer that follows the signations (57): Those who were living without the direction of Christ now accept the mark of his power and love. The study group made the other signations optional (56). They did not appear in the *Roman Ritual* until 1614, but they were very expressive. (In the United States the option has been further promoted by the addition of signations for the hands and feet, unknown before this time.) The members of the study group removed one of the two signations of the forehead, and eliminated the signing of the nostrils because it would not be easily understood. They changed the petition for signing the ears, from the *Roman Ritual's* "that you may hear divine precepts" to the late seventh-century *Gothic Missal's* "that you may hear the voice of the Lord." The petition for the shoulders changed from accepting "the yoke of your service," to one inspired by Matthew 11:30, bearing "the gentle yoke of Christ." The concluding text for signing the whole body was abbreviated. To enhance participation, the study group assigned the signations of the senses to catechists or sponsors and provided an acclamation for the assembly. After the signations, the order no longer refers to the group as "candidates" but as "catechumens," a term first found in Clement of Alexandria.

The imposition of hands was removed for the sake of simplicity. The study group omitted the salt ceremony because its meaning was unclear. "No one understands that the salt of catechumens may be considered as a foretaste of the eucharist." Although antecedents for this ritual were quite ancient, reaching back to Augustine and others in the African and Roman world, only the Western church used salt; its persistence in the West ignored the Eastern traditions. In addition,

> **Assembling publicly for the first time, the candidates who have completed the period of the precatechumenate declare their intention to the Church and the Church, in turn, carrying out its apostolic mission, accepts them as persons who intend to become its members.** *Rite of Christian Initiation of Adults 41*

salt was hard to keep in some regions, and it drew too much attention away from more significant points of the rite.

The giving of a new name may follow the signations, but it is optional (58, 73). This ceremony was included because in some countries those joining non-Christian communities received a new name at the start of their preparation. When the study group heard from African representatives that this custom existed among Muslims, they agreed to permit the giving of a Christian name to catechumens so that they would not appear inferior to their peers joining other religions.

Because some communities had developed a custom of giving a cross or performing some other symbolic action at the beginning of catechumenate formation, the study group permitted this option at the discretion of bishops (59, 74).

The priest then invites the catechumens to enter the church (60). The study group preserved this although it was a late addition to the rite. It appeared about this point in the 1614 ritual, and the 1962 ritual displaced it to the sixth stage. It recalls the importance of the threshold in Peter's conversations with Cornelius. The study group augmented what could have been a sterile entrance by suggesting the use of an appropriate song.

The celebration of the rite of election, which usually coincides with the opening of Lent, also marks the beginning of the period of final, more intense preparation for the sacraments of initiation, during which the elect will be encouraged to follow Christ with greater generosity. *Rite of Christian Initiation of Adults* 118

The celebrant begins the liturgy of the word by telling the catechumens of the dignity of the word of God proclaimed in the church (61). After the readings and the homily, the celebrant may give a book of the gospels to the catechumens (64). The study group remembered the solemn presentation of the gospels from the *Gelasian Sacramentary* and wanted to include something like it here—an optional procession, enthronement and incensation of the book. However, the optional ceremony was simplified to the presentation of the book with a statement like, "Receive the gospel of Jesus Christ, the Son of God." This option offers catechumens the book that will guide their spiritual journey; it seemed more appropriate at the beginning of their formation than near the end, where the *Gelasian* had placed it.

Intercessions for the catechumens follow (65–66). The study group heard some objections that the customary general intercessions seemed unnecessary after these prayers. Consequently the petitions for the catechumens may be augmented with the local community's intentions (65, 68), or the general intercessions and the Creed may both follow the dismissal (in that inverted order), or they may be omitted.

The dismissal of catechumens was restored (67). The study group remained committed to this ancient custom, which is in evidence, for example, in the *Apostolic Constitutions,* over the objections of many in pastoral leadership who thought dismissals appeared inhospitable. The members acquiesced by providing an optional text for situations in which catechumens would not be dismissed, hoping that they would at least move to different seating in the church. But they received support from experimental communities in Togo and Rwanda, for example, who reported success with the dismissals once they implemented them.

During the catechumenate period minor exorcisms (90–94) and blessings (95–97) are provided. The study group permitted the anointing with the oil of catechumens to be given during this period rather than immediately before baptism (98–103). The African church had argued that the oil is needed at the beginning, not the end of baptismal preparation. The inclusion of these prayers attempted to respond to objections that the catechumenate period contained too few rituals. The presentations and ephphetha (see below) were made optional here for the same reasons (21, 104–105). The period of the catechumenate may last several years (7), as in the *Apostolic Tradition.*

© 2000 Passionist Research Center.

Baptistry, St. Agnes Church, Flint, Michigan.

An optional rite of sending catechumens for election appears in American editions (106–117). It was not part of the study group's design. As the Rite of Election moved into cathedrals, many in parish leadership wanted to acknowledge this step in the local community.

PREPARATION FOR BAPTISM

The Rite of Election marks the transition from the period of the catechumenate to that of purification and enlightenment. The study group originally proposed that this ceremony be held within a parish setting, but it developed into a ritual recommended for the cathedral, over which the bishop presided.

The rite unfolds after the homily in these stages: presentation of the catechumens, affirmation by the godparents, invitation and enrollment of names, act of admission or election, intercessions for the elect, prayer over the elect and dismissal of the elect if eucharist follows.

The director of initiation presents the candidates to the bishop or his representative, who invites them forward with their godparents (130–131). He then asks the godparents, "Do you consider these candidates worthy to be admitted to the sacraments of Christian initiation?" "We do," they respond. Godparents thus fulfill their responsibility of vouching for the formation of the catechumens, so evident in sources such as Egeria, John Chrysostom and Caesarius of Arles.

The enrollment may take several forms (132). The study group originally imagined that the presider would write down the names, as Egeria reported the bishop had done; instead, the candidates inscribe their own, or they may call out their names for their godparents or the catechumenate director to write. If there are many names, a list may be prepared beforehand and presented at this time. Godparents may also write their names with the catechumens' in the book of the elect, as attested by Theodore of Mopsuestia and the *Roman-Germanic Pontifical.*

Although the study group at one point proposed that the celebrant should sign the list of names, that suggestion was removed.

In the act of admission or election (133) the celebrant states decisively that the catechumens are among the elect and entrusts them to their godparents. It recalls again the story of Cornelius, where Peter decided the household could be baptized. From here on the order of initiation calls catechumens "the elect," a title drawn from sources as early as the *Apostolic Tradition* and Ambrose, and a distinction of stages as noted in John the Deacon.

Godparents take an active role for the first time in this rite. The order of initiation depends on sponsors to introduce catechumens to the community, but the study group changed the term from here on because "those who brought the candidate as sponsors to the church were less likely to accept the ministry of godparents." The liturgy concludes with intercessions, prayer and dismissal.

The study group restored the scrutinies to what it called their "original place," the Third, Fourth and Fifth Sundays in Lent, at Masses enriched with prayers and readings for the elect. The group also retained the venerable word *scrutiny* over objections that it was hard to translate. Its appearance in Psalm 139 seems to have influenced the decision. Members cautioned that pastoral leaders should not equate *scrutiny* with *examination.* These are rites acclaiming the power of God, as they appeared in Ambrose, not of testing comprehension, as they seemed already in John the Deacon and later in Santori. The study group suppressed the separation of scrutinies for men and women, "because such a distinction offers no legitimate reason for itself," and "above all it no longer corresponds to the mentality of our time." The first draft of the scrutinies still seemed too complicated for many who experimented with them, so they underwent further revision before taking their final form.

The scrutinies have these components: readings, homily, invitation to silent prayer, intercessions for the elect, exorcism, dismissal of the elect and eucharist. When Eucharistic Prayer I is used, the presider may mention the godparents and the elect by name, as the *Gelasian Sacramentary* had requested. The study group omitted the signations formerly in the exorcisms of the *Roman Ritual* to simplify the rite.

The scrutinies are meant to uncover, then heal, all that is weak, defective or sinful in the hearts of the elect; to bring out, then strengthen, all that is upright, strong and good. *Rite of Christian Initiation of Adults* 141

The gospels of the woman at the well, the man born blind and the raising of Lazarus, which originally appeared in the *Würzburg Evangelary* and the Ambrosian missal, were formerly proclaimed from the *Roman Missal* on weekdays in Lent. Now they appear on the scrutiny Sundays of Lent in Year A, and they may be read any year (146). The study group believed that the three gospels outlined a thematic progression in the scrutinies from the personal sin of the Samaritan woman, to the social sin of those who scorned the man born blind, to the radical dimension of evil in death.

After the homily the celebrant invites the elect to bow or kneel in silent prayer (152). The study group originally proposed a third option for posture, prostration, but this was removed. Although the preparatory work assigned the invitations for changing posture to the deacon, the final version of the scrutinies neglected to include his role.

For the intercessions (153), godparents stand with their right hands on the shoulders of the elect. Some petitions are drawn from the *Apostolic Constitutions*, John Chrysostom, the *Gelasian Sacramentary*, the *Roman Ritual* and the petitions of Good Friday; others are inspired by the scriptures assigned for the celebration. As with the Rite of Acceptance, some found all the intercessions repetitive at this Mass; again, the petitions for the elect may be augmented with the local community's intentions (153, 156), or the general intercessions and the Creed may follow (in that inverted order), or they may be omitted.

For the exorcism (154), the celebrant offers a prayer to the Father, with hands joined. He then imposes hands on each of the elect in silence. Then, stretching his hands over the group, he prays to Jesus. A song may follow this prayer. The study group altered this section again and again. Originally they included an exorcism as formerly found in the Gelasian and the *Roman Ritual*, an imprecation directly addressed to the devil. However, many who experimented with the texts found the exorcisms irrelevant to modern sensibilities. Because the complete scrutiny rite already seemed cumbersome, they suggested that the imprecation be removed. The present structure, trinitarian in its movement (prayer addressed to the Father, handlaying for the coming of the Spirit, prayer addressed to Jesus), simplified matters. Essentially, the imprecation addressed to Satan was replaced by a deprecation addressed to Jesus for the same purpose (bidding evil to be gone), but the section is still titled "exorcism," even though it changed what exorcisms used to be. A song and dismissal of the elect conclude the scrutiny (155). The second and third scrutinies (164–170; 171–177) follow in the same manner.

While fashioning the presentations, the study group decided to limit them to two: the Creed (a ritual that had appeared in Ambrose) and the Lord's Prayer (which emerged in Augustine). They did so for several reasons. These enjoyed more antiquity than other presentations, such as that of a Bible. Besides, some catechumens were illiterate; others might believe the Bible possessed magical properties after such a treatment; the Lord's Prayer and the Creed already act as a summary of sacred scripture; and the presentation of a Bible seemed more appropriate to the Rite of Acceptance.

The occasion for the presentations is flexible. Since the Sundays of Lent were already crowded with scrutinies, the study group recommended that the presentations be celebrated on weekdays, at Masses when the faithful could be present (157). The members clearly preferred that the presentation of the Creed follow the first scrutiny and that of the Lord's Prayer follow the third. The Creed traditionally formed a point of reference for prebaptismal catechesis (as it did, for example, for Cyril of Jerusalem), and the group thought that the Lord's Prayer should be handed on only after the third scrutiny, as baptism drew near. Many experimenting with the rites, however, complained that they offered too many rituals for the period of purification and enlightenment and too few for the period of the catechumenate. Consequently, the study group permitted these to be anticipated (21), but not before catechumens were ready for them (104). In those cases, the ephphetha could conclude each of the presentations if it were not to be offered during the preparatory rites on Holy Saturday morning (105). Furthermore, the order of initiation permits the presentation of the Lord's Prayer to be deferred to Holy Saturday morning (149, 185), which unites it with the day of the recitation of the Creed, in the tradition of Augustine.

The presentation of the Creed includes these parts (157–163): readings, homily, presentation of the Creed, prayer over the elect and dismissal of the elect. The Creed is presented when the faithful recite it for the catechumens (160). In keeping with the tradition of the protected nature of this text, shared only with those to whom it was explained, the study group never mentioned presenting the elect with a written version of the Creed. The elect are expected to commit the Creed to memory (148).

The presentation of the Lord's Prayer follows a similar structure (178–184): readings, homily, prayer over the elect and dismissal of the elect. The presentation of the Lord's Prayer occurs in the proclamation of the gospel passage that recounts Jesus teaching his followers how to pray. Augustine had reported the presentation in just this way.

The preparatory rites were established for Holy Saturday morning, in keeping with the *Apostolic Tradition,* after some interest in offering Good Friday as an alternative, as in the testimony of John Chrysostom. The rites include the ephphetha (197–199) and the recitation of the Creed (193–196) and, optionally, choosing a baptismal name (200–202) and the presentation of the Lord's Prayer (149, 185). The ceremony concludes with a prayer of blessing and dismissal (203–205).

The study group decided not to include the renunciation and anointing, which occurred separate from baptism possibly as early as Theodore of Mopsuestia, but more clearly in Caesarius of Arles and the *Gelasian Sacramentary.* They felt the renunciation should remain with the profession of faith immediately before baptism.

The members of the group removed from the ephphetha the use of saliva, "which seems to be intolerable everywhere on earth." In place of signing the nostrils, the celebrant now signs the closed lips of the elect (199). The formula was adjusted accordingly, and now makes a more direct reference to Jesus' healing of the man whose hearing and speech were impaired (Mark 7:31–37). The study group decided not to include a recitation of the Lord's Prayer; this custom, intimated by Augustine, had appeared very late in the tradition (the *Roman-Germanic Pontifical*). In addition, they believed that the Lord's Prayer belongs to the Christian assembly, so the newly baptized should recite it with the whole assembly at the baptismal eucharist.

The entire community is urged to fast with those to be baptized (185; cf. CSL 110), a custom as old as the *Didache.*

The third step in the Christian initiation of adults is the celebration of the sacraments of baptism, confirmation, and eucharist. Through this final step the elect, receiving pardon for their sins, are admitted into the people of God. They are graced with adoption as children of God and are led by the Holy Spirit into the promised fullness of time begun in Christ and, as they share in the eucharistic sacrifice and meal, even to a foretaste of the kingdom of God. *Rite of Christian Initiation of Adults* 206

BAPTISM

Several changes were made in the rites of initiation. The entire rite of baptism was moved to a new place in the liturgy. Formerly, baptisms were celebrated after the readings from the Old Testament (concluding the Vigil service), and before the Glory to God and the New Testament readings (starting the Easter Mass). In the revised liturgy, the baptismal rite was moved in its entirety to a position after the homily, pressing more closely together the proclamation of all the scriptures.

The order of initiation includes the presentation of the candidates, invitation to prayer, litany of the saints, prayer over the water, renunciation of sin, profession of faith, baptism, clothing with a baptismal garment, presentation of a lighted candle, confirmation and eucharist. The litany of the saints (221) can be traced to baptisms in the *Gelasian Sacramentary*. The prayer over the water (222), a baptismal rite introduced by Tertullian, was prepared by another study group, simplified and supported with optional texts. The renunciation of sin now immediately precedes the profession of faith (223–225). However, the study group permitted variations on the text and invited local adaptation in naming the sin to be renounced.

At the profession of faith, the godparents may give the names of each to be baptized to the celebrant (225), as they did in the *Roman Pontifical* of the twelfth century. The anointing that preceded this profession was removed to simplify the baptismal rites. The question about belief in Christ has been amplified in the revised rite of baptism. The priest following the 1614 ritual asked, "Do you believe in Jesus Christ, his only Son, our Lord, who was born and suffered?" The study group returned to a version of the question posed in the *Apostolic Tradition:* "Do you believe in Jesus Christ, his only Son, our Lord, who was born of the Virgin Mary, was crucified, died, and was buried, rose from the dead, and is now seated at the right hand of the Father?"

The order of initiation still entrusts baptism to the ministry of the bishop (12, 207), as Ignatius of Antioch preferred at the beginning of the second century. Others, of course, share this ministry.

The study group restored baptism by immersion, which the 1962 rubrics had omitted, and placed it ahead of the option for pouring "to observe the order of dignity." The celebrant immerses or pours water three times while reciting the formula which first appeared in Matthew's gospel, in the tradition established from the *Roman-Germanic Pontifical*. The order no longer requires pouring water in the form of a cross. Although nudity had been specified at least from the time of the *Apostolic Tradition* through that of John the Deacon, the order now cautions that in the case of immersion "decency and decorum should be preserved" (226).

The white garment, in evidence from the time of Ambrose if not also of John of Jerusalem, became an optional rite (229). The formula that accompanies it underwent a few revisions. It now addresses the newly baptized, using their name as Christians for the first time. To highlight the paschal character of this eschatological ritual, the formula was amended to include references to 2 Corinthians 5:17 and Galatians 3:27.

The newly baptized also receive a candle (230), keeping the tradition noted first in the East by Gregory of Nazianzen and Proclus of Constantinople. The formula from the *Roman Ritual* was adapted to include a reference to Ephesians 5:8, again to highlight the paschal character of this eschatological rite.

Since the Second Vatican Council, the presbyter who baptizes an adult has the faculty to confirm that person immediately. The request, supported by the study group, came from a pan-African conference of catechists, who argued that it would honor the ancient and Eastern traditions, serve the pastoral needs of adults who had to wait for confirmation, follow the recent evolution of discipline which accorded the faculty to confirm to priests in certain circumstances including danger of death, and respond to the request in the *Constitution on the Sacred Liturgy* (71) that confirmation be more closely linked to the whole of initiation.

Now, according to the *Code of Canon Law* (885 §2), "a presbyter who has this faculty [to confirm] must use it for those in whose favor the faculty was granted."

> **[Mystagogy] is a time for the community and the neophytes together to grow in deepening their grasp of the paschal mystery and in making it part of their lives through meditation on the gospel, sharing in the eucharist, and doing works of charity.** *Rite of Christian Initiation of Adults 244*

This decision, recommended by the study group, posed a difficulty in the administration of the post-baptismal anointings. The *Roman Ritual* called for the priest to anoint the crown of the head of the newly baptized with chrism; later, a bishop would confirm the forehead with chrism. The double anointing had been part of the Roman church since the *Apostolic Tradition*. Now the members were afraid that the difference between the two anointings would blur. To avoid the kind of duplication disparaged by the liturgical principles of the Second Vatican Council, the first anointing is now eliminated when confirmation follows immediately (228).

The Rite of Confirmation, which at times called for the bishop to lay hands on each candidate, now calls for an extension of his hands over them all (234). The study group proposed having each candidate come individually to the priest and kneel for handlaying, but this was not included in the final rite. They also planned that the prayer for the sevenfold gift of the Holy Spirit would be interrupted with several acclamations of "Amen" from the assembly; this too disappeared from the published rite.

The newly baptized approach the eucharist in the same celebration, a practice first witnessed by Justin. The celebrant gives an introduction to communion as the climax of initiation (243), a rubric the study group included because of its appearance in the *Apostolic Tradition*.

LIFE AFTER INITIATION

Mystagogy takes place primarily on the Sundays of the Easter season (247). The newly baptized now share regularly in the eucharist and deepen their grasp of the paschal mystery with the community. A celebration near Pentecost could close this period, and on the anniversary of baptism the new Christians could celebrate again (249). The bishop may celebrate a Mass with the neophytes sometime during the year (251).

In recommending Sundays for mystagogy the study group changed the course used in the early church. The *Apostolic Tradition* (where a mystagogic catechesis first emerges), Egeria, John of Jerusalem, Ambrose, Augustine, John

Chrysostom and Theodore of Mopsuestia all reported that the bishop gave instructions during the octave of Easter. Beginning with the *Gelasian Sacramentary*, the newly baptized were urged to attend the daily eucharist that week. The texts for daily Mass during the octave of Easter still make frequent reference to the presence of the newly baptized, but the order of initiation no longer specifically recommends their attendance.

The idea for a celebration near Pentecost came from groups that had experimented with the revised rites. They thought the period of mystagogy needed closure, and some recommended that confirmation be moved there. The study group believed "it would be regrettable if the place of confirmation were determined only as a function of pastoral pragmatism"; the final text permits such a move only for a "serious reason" (24).

Above all, the study group had in mind that mystagogy would involve an immersion in the community. The priest, the entire community and the godparents would continually invite the newly baptized into their life (248).

Considering the task that lay before Balthasar Fischer and Study Group 22, one is struck by how much of the ancient catechumenate they restored, integrated and presented to the church in such a short time, in a fresh way, accommodated to the era and adaptable to diverse places. One measure of its success is the development of parallel catechumenates in other Christian churches, for example, *Living Witnesses: The Adult Catechumenate* (Winnipeg: The Evangelical Lutheran Church in Canada, 1992); *Come to the Waters* (Nashville: Discipleship Resources, 1996) for the United Methodist Church; and *Welcome to Christ* (Minneapolis: Augsburg Fortress, 1997) for the Evangelical Lutheran Church in America.

◆◆◆

First Interest

• People express interest after hearing the mystery of Christ proclaimed.

Catechesis

• Those inquiring into the Christian faith become catechumens through an opening dialogue, the acceptance of the gospel, the affirmation by sponsors and the assembly, signations and an invitation to hear the word of God.

• During their period of formation they receive catechesis, become familiar with the Christian way of life, participate in liturgical rites and spread the gospel.

• Word services during this period may include an anointing with the oil of catechumens.

Preparation for Baptism

• Catechumens begin their proximate preparation for baptism at the Rite of Election, a ceremony including the presentation of the catechumens, the affirmation by the godparents and the assembly, the invitation and enrollment of names, and the act of admission or election.

- During the period of purification and enlightenment the elect make a more intense spiritual preparation, aided by scrutinies and the presentations.

- The scrutinies include an invitation to silent prayer, intercessions for the elect and an exorcism.

- In the presentations the elect receive the Creed from the assembly of the faithful and the Lord's Prayer from the proclamation of the gospel.

Baptism

- Baptism is preceded by the preparation rites on Holy Saturday, which may include the ephphetha and the recitation of the Creed.

- The baptismal rite takes place in a parish church during the Easter Vigil and includes a presentation of the candidates, an invitation to prayer, a litany of the saints, a prayer over the water, the renunciation of sin and profession of faith, baptism, the white garment, the lighted candle, confirmation and the first reception of eucharist.

Life after Initiation

- The newly baptized continue their formation by celebrating and reflecting on the rites during mystagogy.

- They integrate into the Christian community.

- They may celebrate eucharist with the bishop sometime during the year.

You ◆ 32
Reader and Voyager

Everyone who travels the highway of the catechumenate experiences death and resurrection. Easter, the great celebration of the rising of Jesus to new life, embraces those who die to their former allegiances and rise to give their hearts to Christ.

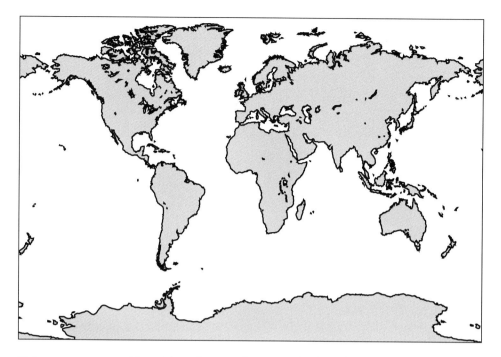

But as you can see, it's not just the catechumen who has died and risen. The catechumenate itself died and rose. Practiced for the first five centuries with local adaptations throughout the centers of the Christian world, it went dormant because it succeeded. So many people had become Christian that most of those remaining to be baptized were infants. Pastorally adapted again, it collapsed into a lengthy set of prayers and rituals without its catechetical support. But when the need for prebaptismal catechesis returned in the missionary outreach of a newly global church, the catechumenate made a slow but deliberate comeback, overcoming the odds of poverty, exile and the misunderstanding that resulted from the well-intentioned standards of tradition, charity and obedience. Through the work of the Holy Spirit guiding the Second Vatican Council the catechumenate rose again.

The death and resurrection story of the catechumenate offers hope to all those who walk in faith. Some basic goodness in its bones allowed it to endure the temptations and grace of its own highway.

Travel always brings change, not just in scenery but in the traveler. And not just in the traveler, but in all those the traveler touches. When the catechumenate rose in the post–Vatican II church, we all were changed because it invited us into evangelization, catechesis, worship, community and service in a transformed way. When any catechumen is baptized at the end of the highway, change comes to that person, but also to you and me. Our lives are enriched whenever we behold the divine touch of grace.

So, you, wherever you are—traveling the highway, giving directions, offering refreshments or observing from the stands—the catechumen's journey is also about you. You will find delight in God and hope in the midst of suffering whenever you see a catechumen. You can't miss them. They're the ones holding the staff of faith, following the map of God's word with cross as compass and an entire community as guide. Eyes lifted up, hearts brimming with love, they open their lips to sing their joy as they step with confidence onto the path of endless promise, the Hallelujah Highway.

BIBLIOGRAPHY

General Sources

Cavallotto, Giuseppe. *Catechumenato antico: Diventare cristiani secondo i padri*. Bologna: Edizione Dehoniane Bologna, 1996.

_____, ed. *Iniziazione cristiana e catecumenato: Divenire cristiani per essere battezzati*. Bologna: Edizione Dehoniane Bologna, 1996.

Dujarier, Michel. *A History of the Catechumenate: The First Six Centuries*. Trans. Edward J. Hassl. New York: Sadlier, 1979.

_____. *Le parrainage des adultes aux trois premiers siécles de l'église: Récherche historique sur l'évolution des garanties et des étapes catéchuménales avant 313*. Parole et Mission. Paris: Les Éditions du Cerf, 1962.

Johnson, Maxwell. *The Rites of Christian Initiation: Their Evolution and Interpretation*. Collegeville: Liturgical Press, 1999.

Made, Not Born: New Perspectives on Christian Initiation and the Catechumenate. Liturgical Studies. Notre Dame: University of Notre Dame Press, 1976.

Maertens, Thierry. *Histoire et pastorale du rituel du catéchuménat et du baptême*. Paroisse et Liturgie: Collection de Pastorale Liturgique 56. Bruges: Biblica, 1962.

Mazza, Enrico. *Mystagogy*. New York: Pueblo Publishing Company, 1989.

Saxer, Victor. *Les rites de l'initiation chrétienne du IIe au VIe siécle: esquisse historique et signification d'après leurs principaux témoins*. Spoleto: Centro Italiano de Studi Sull'Alto Medioevo, 1988.

Whitaker, E. C. *Documents of the Baptismal Liturgy*. London: SPCK, 1960.

Yarnold, Edward. *The Awe-Inspiring Rites of Initiation: The Origins of the RCIA*. 2nd ed. Collegeville: Liturgical Press, 1994.

Chapter 2: Peter

Acts of the Apostles 2:10–11.

1 Peter 1–3.

Fuller, Reginald H. "Christian Initiation in the New Testament." *Made, Not Born: New Perspectives on Christian Initiation and the Catechumenate*, 7–31. Notre Dame: University of Notre Dame Press, 1976.

Chapter 3: Paul

Acts of the Apostles 9; 13; 22.

Letter to the Romans 6.

Beasley-Murray, G. R. *Baptism in the New Testament*. London: Macmillan & Co., Ltd. 1963.

Chapter 4: Didache

The Didache, or the Teaching of the Twelve Apostles. Ancient Christian Writers 6, 3–25. Westminster, Maryland: Newman Press, 1948.

Finn, Thomas M. *Early Christian Baptism and the Catechumenate: West and East Syria*. Message of the Fathers of the Church 5, 32–6. A Michael Glazier Book. Collegeville: Liturgical Press, 1992.

Rordorf, Willy. "Baptism according to the *Didache*." *The Didache in Modern Research*. Ed. Jonathan A. Draper, 212–22. Leiden: E. J. Brill, 1996.

Chapter 5: Justin

Finn, Thomas M. *Early Christian Baptism and the Catechumenate: West and East Syria*. Message of the Fathers of the Church 6, 36–41. A Michael Glazier Book. Collegeville: Liturgical Press, 1992.

Justin Martyr. *The First and Second Apologies*. Trans. Leslie William Barnard. Ancient Christian Writers 26. New York: Paulist Press, 1997.

Story, Cullen I. K. "Justin's *Apology* I 62–64: Its Importance for the Author's Treatment of Christian Baptism." *Vigiliae Christianae* 16 (1962): 172–8.

Chapter 6: Clement of Alexandria

Clement of Alexandria. *The Instructor. The Stromata, or Miscellanies*. in *The Ante-Nicene Fathers*, vol. 2. American Reprint of the Edinburgh Edition. Grand Rapids: Wm. B. Eerdmans Publishing Company, 1989.

Finn, Thomas M. *Early Christian Baptism and the Catechumenate: Italy, North Africa and Egypt*. Message of the Fathers of the Church 6, 180–91. A Michael Glazier Book. Collegeville: Liturgical Press, 1992.

Norris, Richard. "The Result of the Loss of Baptismal Discipline." *The Baptismal Mystery and the Catechumenate*. Ed. Michael W. Merriman, 20–35. New York: Church Hymnal Corporation, 1990.

Chapter 7: Tertullian

Finn, Thomas M. *Early Christian Baptism and the Catechumenate: Italy, North Africa and Egypt*. Message of the Fathers of the Church 6, 115–28. A Michael Glazier Book. Collegeville: Liturgical Press, 1992.

The Passion of Perpetua and Felicity; Sermons of S. Augustine Upon These Texts. Trans. W. H. Shewring. London: Sheed & Ward, 1931.

Rankin, David. *Tertullian and the Church*. Cambridge: University Press, 1995.

Tertullian. *Tertullian's Homily on Baptism.* Trans. Ernest Evans. London: SPCK, 1964.

Tertullian. *Against Marcion. Apology. The Crown. To the Nations. Prescription Against Heresies. Repentance. The Resurrection of the Flesh.* in *The Ante-Nicene Fathers,* vol. 3. American Reprint of the Edinburgh Edition. Grand Rapids: Wm. B. Eerdmans Publishing Company, 1989.

Chapter 8: Origen

Origen. *Against Celsus. Principles.* in *The Ante-Nicene Fathers,* vol. 4. American Reprint of the Edinburgh Edition. Grand Rapids: Wm. B. Eerdmans Publishing Company, 1989.

_____. *Homilies on Genesis and Exodus.* Trans. Ronald E. Heine. Washington: Catholic University of America Press, 1982.

Chapter 9: Apostolic Tradition

Bradshaw, Paul F. "Redating the Apostolic Tradition: Some Preliminary Steps" in *Rule of Prayer, Rule of Faith: Essays in Honor of Aidan Kavanagh, OSB,* 3–17. A Pueblo Book. Collegeville: Liturgical Press, 1996.

Cuming, Geoffrey J. *Hippolytus: A Text for Students, with Introduction, Translation, Commentary and Notes.* Bramcote Notts: Grove Books, 1984.

Elvira (Illiberitanum), Council of (309). *Sacrorum conciliorum nova et amplissima collectio.* Ed. Johannes Dominicus Mansi et al. Vol. 2. Florence: Antonius Zatta Venetus, 1759.

Finn, Thomas M. *Early Christian Baptism and the Catechumenate: Italy, North Africa and Egypt.* Message of the Fathers of the Church 6, 45–51. A Michael Glazier Book. Collegeville: Liturgical Press, 1992.

Metzger, Marcel. "Nouvelles perspectives pour la pretendue Tradition Apostolique." *Ecclesia Orans* 5 (1988) 3:241–259.

Pseudo-Clement. *Recognitionum 3:67. Patrologiae cursus completus.* Ed. Jacques-Paul Migne. Vol. 1. Series Graeca. Paris: J-P. Migne, 1857.

Chapter 10: Apostolic Constitutions

Constitutions of the Holy Apostles in *The Ante-Nicene Fathers,* vol. 7. American Reprint of the Edinburgh Edition. Grand Rapids: Wm. B. Eerdmans Publishing Company, 1989.

Finn, Thomas M. *Early Christian Baptism and the Catechumenate: West and East Syria.* Message of the Fathers of the Church 5, 55–60. A Michael Glazier Book. Collegeville: Liturgical Press, 1992.

Chapter 11: Egeria

Cyril of Jerusalem. *Lenten Lectures. Mystagogical Lectures.* in *The Fathers of the Church,* vol. 2. Washington: Catholic University of America Press, 1970.

Egeria's Travels to the Holy Land. Trans. John Wilkinson. Jerusalem: Ariel, 1981.

Finn, Thomas M. *Early Christian Baptism and the Catechumenate: West and East Syria.* Message of the Fathers of the Church 5, 41–55. A Michael Glazier Book. Collegeville: Liturgical Press, 1992.

Chapter 12: Ambrose

Babut, Ernest Charles. *La plus ancienne décrétale.* Paris: Société nouvelle de librairie et d'édition, 1904.

Yarnold, Edward. *The Awe-Inspiring Rites of Initiation: The Origins of the RCIA.* 2nd ed. Collegeville: Liturgical Press, 1994.

Chapter 13: Augustine

Augustine. *The First Catechetical Instruction [De catechizandis-rudibus].* Trans. Joseph P. Christopher. Ancient Christian Writers 2. Westminster, Maryland: Newman Bookshop, 1946.

_____. *On Faith and Works* in *Ancient Christian Writers.* Trans. Gregory J. Lombardo. New York: Newman Press, 1988.

_____. *Sermons. The Works of Saint Augustine: A Translation for the 21st Century.* Trans. Edmund Hill. Brooklyn: New City Press, 1990.

Harmless, William. *Augustine and the Catechumenate.* A Pueblo Book. Collegeville: Liturgical Press, 1995.

Chapter 14: John Chrysostom

Yarnold, Edward. *The Awe-Inspiring Rites of Initiation: The Origins of the RCIA.* 2nd ed. Collegeville: Liturgical Press, 1994.

Chapter 15: Theodore of Mopsuestia

Yarnold, Edward. *The Awe-Inspiring Rites of Initiation: The Origins of the RCIA.* 2nd ed. Collegeville: Liturgical Press, 1994.

Chapter 16: Pseudo-Dionysius the Areopagite

Pseudo-Dionysius: The Complete Works. Trans. Colm Luibheid. The Classics of Western Spirituality. New York: Paulist Press, 1987.

Chapter 17: John the Deacon

Finn, Thomas M. *Early Christian Baptism and the Catechumenate: Italy, North Africa and Egypt.* Message of the Fathers of the Church 6, 84–9. A Michael Glazier Book. Collegeville: Liturgical Press, 1992.

Chapter 18: Caesarius of Arles

Saint Caesarius of Arles: Sermons. Trans. Mary Magdeleine Mueller. Vol. I. New York: Fathers of the Church, Inc., 1956.

_____. Vols. II and III. Washington: Catholic University of America Press, 1964, 1973.

Chapters 19–23: The Sacramentaries and Pontificals

Alcuin. "Epistolae" 110. MGH. *Ep Epistolae Karolini* aevi 4/2:158f.

Durandus, William. *Le pontifical romain au moyen-âge: Le pontifical de Guillaume Durande.* Ed. Michel Andrieu. Studi e Testi 88.

Handbook for Liturgical Studies. I. Introduction to the Liturgy. The Pontifical Liturgical Institute. Ed. Anscar J. Chupungco. Collegeville: Liturgical Press, 1997.

Liber sacramentorum Romanae aeclesiae ordinis anni circuli (Sacramentarium Gelasianum). Ed. Leo Cunibert Mohlberg. Rerum Ecclesiasticarum Documenta. Series maior, Fontes IV. Rome: Casa Editrice Herder, 1981.

McBrien, Richard P. *Lives of the Popes: The Pontiffs from St. Peter to John Paul II.* HarperSanFrancisco, 1997.

Missale Gothicum. Vat. Reg. lat. 317. Ed. Leo Cunibert Mohlbert. Rerum Ecclesiasticarum Documenta. Series Maior, Fontes V. Rome: Casa Editrice Herder, 1961.

Nocent, Adrian. *The Liturgical Year. Volume 2, Lent.* Trans. Matthew J. O'Connell. Collegeville: Liturgical Press, 1977.

Ordo XI. Les ordines Romain du haut moyen-âge. Ed. Michel Andrieu. Vol. 23 *ff.* Louvain: Spicilegium Sacrum Lovaniense Administration, 1960.

Pontifical romain au moyen-âge: Le pontifical de la curie romaine au xiiie siècle. Ed. Michel Andrieu. Studi e Testi 87.

Pontificale Romano-Germanicum. Ed. Cyrille Vogel and Reinhard Elze. Studi e Testi 226, 227 and 269.

Pontificale Romanum saeculi xii: Le pontifical romain au moyen-âge. Ed. Michel Andrieu. Studi e Testi 86 *ff,* 99.

Sacramentarium Bergomense: Manoscritto del secolo IX della Biblioteca di S. Alessandro in Colonna in Bergamo. Monumenta Bergomensia VI, 109–110, 129–130, 137–138. Transcribed by Angelo Paredi, tables by Giuseppe Fasi. Bergamo: Edizioni "Monumenta Bergomensia," 1962.

Chapter 24: Toribio Motolinía

Basalenque, Diego. *Historia de la Provincia de San Nicolás de Tolentino de Michoacán del Orden de N. P. S. Agustín.* Colección México Heroico, 18. Mexico: Editorial Jus, 1963.

Beckmann, J. "L'initiation et la célébration baptismale dans les missions du 16e siècle a nos jours." *La Maison-Dieu* 58 (1959) 2:48–70.

Códice Franciscano. Siglo XVI. Nueva coleccion de documentos para la historia de Mexico. Mexico City: Salvador Chavez Hayhoe, 1941.

Icazbalceta, Joaquin Garcia. *Juan de Zumárraga: Primer Obispo y Arzobispo de México.* Mexico City: Antiqua Libreria de Andrade y Morales, 1881.

Lara, Jaime. "'Precious Green Jade Water': A Sixteenth-Century Adult Catechumenate in the New World." *Worship* 71 (September, 1997)/5:415–428.

"Manuale sacramentorum, 1560." Ed. Jakob Baumgartner. *Mission und Liturgie in Mexiko,* vol. 2. Schöneck/Beckenried (Switzerland): Administration der Neuen Zeitschrift für Missionswissenschaft, 1972.

Motolinía, Toribio. *History of the Indians of New Spain.* Trans. Elizabeth Andros Foster. New Mexico: Cortés Society, 1950.

Póu y Marti, José Maria. "El Libro perdido de las platicas ocoloquios de los doce primeros misioneros de Mexico." *Scrittidi Storia e Paleografia.* Miscellanea Francesco Ehrle. Vol. 3, 281–333. Studi e Testi 39. Rome: Biblioteca Apostolica Vaticana, 1924.

Ricard, Robert. *The Spiritual Conquest of Mexico: An Essay on the Apostolate and the Evangelizing Methods of the Mendicant Orders in New Spain: 1523–1572.* Trans. Lesley Byrd Simpson. Berkeley & Los Angeles: University of California Press, 1966.

Tobar, Balthasar de. *Compendio Bulario Indico.* Ed. Manuel Gutierrez de Arce. Vol. 1. Seville: Escuela de estudios Hispano-Americanos de Sevilla, 1954.

Chapter 25: Alessandro Valignano

Christaens, J. "L'organisation d'un catéchuménat au 16e siècle." *La Maison-Dieu* 58 (1959) 2:71–82.

De Forest, John H. *Sunrise in the Sunrise Kingdom.* New York: Young People's Missionary Movement of the United States and Canada, 1909.

Gay, Jesús López. *El Catechumenado en la mision del Japon del s. XVI.* Studia Missionalia. Documenta et opera. Rome: Libreria dell'Universitá Gregoriana, 1966.

Jennes, Joseph. *A History of the Catholic Church in Japan from its Beginnings to the Early Meiji Period (1549–1873).* Missionary Bulletin Series #8. Tokyo: Committee of the Apostolate, 1959.

Moran, J. F. *The Japanese and the Jesuits: Alessandro Valignano in Sixteenth-Century Japan.* London and New York: Routledge, 1993.

Ross, Andrew C. *A Vision Betrayed: The Jesuits in Japan and China 1542–1742.* Maryknoll: Orbis Books, 1994.

Valignano, Alexandro. *Il Cerimoniale per i missionari del Giappone.* Ed. Giuseppe Fr. Schütte. Rome: Edizioni di "Storia e letteratura," 1946.

Chapter 26: Giulio Santori

Christaens, J. "L'organisation d'un catéchuménat au 16e siècle." *La Maison-Dieu* 58 (1959) 2:71–82.

Zanon, Giuseppe. "L'iniziazione cristiana secondo il Rituale del Santori." *Iniziazione cristiana e catecumenato: Divenire cristiani per essere battezzati* 169–96. Bologna: Edizione Dehoniane Bologna, 1996.

Chapter 27: The Roman Ritual

Rituale Romanum. Rome: Typis Societatis S. Joannis Evangelistae Desclée & Cie, 1952.

Chapter 28: Louis-Simon Faurie

Beckmann, J. "L'initiation et la célébration baptismale dans les missions du 16e siècle a nos jours." *La Maison-Dieu* 58 (1959) 2:48–70.

Collectanea S. Congregationis de Propaganda Fide seu Decreta instructiones rescripta pro apostolicis missionibus. Rome: Polyglot Press, 1907. 1:97, 155, 391, 397, 403, 713.

Launay, Adrien. *Histoire des Missions de Chine: Mission du Kouy-Tcheou.* Société des missions-étrangères, 1907–1908. I:154–157, II:409–414.

Chapter 29: Charles Lavigerie

Beckmann, J. "L'initiation et la célébration baptismale dans les missions du 16e siècle a nos jours." *La Maison-Dieu* 58 (1959) 2:48–70.

Rommelaere, André. "La préparation au baptême dans les missions de l'Afrique noire." *Nouvelle revue de science missionnaire* 6 (1950): 127–135; 161–174.

Chapter 30: Joseph Blomjous

"Additiones et variationes in Rituali Romano circa ordinem baptismi adultorum." *Acta Apostolicae Sedis* 54: 310–338.

Gouzi, Paulette. "Le catéchuménat d'adultes en milieu déchristianisé." *La Maison-Dieu* 2 (1945): 52–69.

Martimor, Aimé-Georges. "Catéchuménat et initiation chrétienne des adultes par étapes: Jalons historiques." *Notitiae* 21/228–229 (1985): 382–93.

Seumois, Xavier. "La structure de la liturgie baptismale romaine et les problèmes du catéchuménat missionnaire." *La Maison-Dieu* 58 (1959): 83–110.

Chapter 31: Balthasar Fischer

Coetus a studiis 22: De Sacramentis. Consilium ad exsequendam constitutionem de sacra liturgia. *Schemata, Rite of Christian Initiation of Adults.* 1965–69. Care of Hesburgh Library, University of Notre Dame.

Fischer, Balthasar. "The Rite of Christian Initiation of Adults: Rediscovery and New Beginnings." *Worship* 64/2 (March, 1990): 98–106.

Hughes, Kathleen. *How Firm a Foundation: Voices of the Early Liturgical Movement.* Chicago: Liturgy Training Publications, 1990.

Kavanagh, Aidan. "Christian Initiation in Post-Conciliar Roman Catholicism: A Brief Report." *Studia Liturgica* 12/2–3 (1977): 107–15.

Rite of Christian Initiation of Adults. International Commission on English in the Liturgy and Bishops' Committee on the Liturgy. Chicago: Liturgy Training Publications, 1988.

INDICES